'*Tools for Reflective Ministry* provides a wealth of resources for people involved in various forms of ministry who want to be reflective practitioners. Sally and Paul Nash summarize and synthesize the contributions of many teachers and guides and offer an impressive array of ideas, strategies, tools, questions, insights, practices, examples and exercises to stimulate and equip us. A resource book to plunder again and again, alone and with others.'

Stuart Murray Williams, Urban Expression

'A really welcome and helpful resource written with knowledge, understanding and wisdom by reflective practitioners who live what they teach.'

Roy Searle, Leader, Northumbria Community

'Winsome and inviting, this practical, inspirational book is an invaluable help to all who would dive beneath the surface of themselves. Well researched, but never wooden, it is a feast for all who lament the famine of reflection that blights those of us who feel stranded in a soundbite culture.'

Jeff Lucas, author, speaker and broadcaster

'*Tools for Reflective Ministry* is a gem of a resource for practitioners. By staying closely rooted to the practice of ministry, Sally and Paul Nash have produced an invaluable addition to the growing literature on theological reflection.'

Pete Ward, Senior Lecturer in Youth Ministry and
Theological Education, King's College London

'For those of us who would welcome help in being able to reflect well, Paul and Sally's book will be invaluable. They have much to say to help us individually, and with others, to develop habits of recognition that see and hear God's action and voice every day we live. They write personally and professionally, distilling an enormous amount of contemporary wisdom clearly and accessibly. I warmly commend these "tools" that they have brought together for our good.'

Keith Sinclair, Bishop of Birkenhead

'As the language of theological reflection and reflective practice becomes increasingly a part of our lexicon, many practitioners in ministry will be asking, "How do I actually go about doing this?" This book provides some much needed help and practical advice for empowering practitioners in their Christian discipleship. This is an invaluable text!'

Dr Anthony G. Reddie, Research Fellow in Black Theological Studies
for the British Methodi͏̈ ͏̈ ͏̈ ͏̈ the Queen's Foundation
on

'Those of us who have the privilege of knowing and working with Sally and Paul Nash recognize their distinctive skills as individuals and their complementary skills as married professional colleagues. In this engaging, theoretically grounded and thoroughly practical book, they invite us, the readers, to enter their theologically informed world and in so doing to become better theologically informed reflective practitioners ourselves.'

Leslie J. Francis, Professor of Religions and Education, University of Warwick and Canon Theologian, Bangor Cathedral

'A fabulous resource, thoroughly practical and deeply inspiring, and born out of the accumulated wisdom gained from personal commitment to the discipline of reflection. Not only do the authors make accessible and comprehensible the disciplines of reflection even to the absolute beginner, but they also provide stacks of practical help and techniques to enable all to grow in this most vital practice. Making available to a wider constituency the fruit of their years of study and teaching in this area, Paul and Sally Nash have done the church a great service in contributing in this way to the development of deeper people.'

Ian Parkinson, Vicar of All Saints' Church Marple and team leader, New Wine North & East

'In my work I find that increasingly reflective practice is a key tool for discipling and inviting young people to make real progress in their journey of faith. Paul and Sally's book has not only further equipped me for this role but also deepened my understanding of the vitality that can be brought to a person's spirituality through this crucial area of ministry.'

Jason Gardner, Youth Project Researcher, London Institute for Contemporary Christianity

'This book is a skilful blend of sound theory, creative practice and perceptive stories that uncover the riches of reflective ministry. Sally and Paul generously share insights from their experience of reflective practice, both in their own lives and in their ministry in different contexts. This is a book to read and to treasure, to return to again and again for new tools to unlock the huge potential for learning and growth in our everyday experiences.'

Jenny Baker, writer and co-founder of the Sophia Network for women in youth work

Dr Sally Nash is Director of the Midlands Centre for Youth Ministry, a partnership between St John's, Nottingham, and Youth for Christ. She has been involved in Youth for Christ for over 25 years in the training and support of youth workers. Her publications include *A Theology for Urban Youth Work* and *Sustaining Your Spirituality*.

The Revd Paul Nash is Senior Chaplain at Birmingham Children's Hospital and a tutor at the Midlands Centre for Youth Ministry. His first ministry experience was with Youth for Christ and when he left to be ordained he was part of the leadership team. He is involved in a number of community and church projects as well as chaplaincy. He was the initiator of the Grove Youth Series and has written *What Theology for Youth Work?*

Paul and Sally were married in 1986 and have worked and ministered together for most of that time. They are the authors (with Jo Pimlott) of *Skills for Collaborative Ministry* (SPCK, 2008). They are complete opposites on the Myers Briggs® Type Indicator (ESFP and INTJ) and have both fruitful and challenging times reflecting together.

SPCK Library of Ministry

COMMUNITY AND MINISTRY: AN INTRODUCTION TO
COMMUNITY DEVELOPMENT IN A CHRISTIAN CONTEXT
Paul Ballard and Lesley Husselbee

PIONEER MINISTRY: HELPING TO BUILD A
MIXED-ECONOMY CHURCH
Angela Shier-Jones

READER MINISTRY EXPLORED
Cathy Rowling and Paula Gooder

SKILLS FOR COLLABORATIVE MINISTRY
Sally Nash, Jo Pimlott and Paul Nash

SUPPORTING NEW MINISTERS IN THE LOCAL CHURCH:
A HANDBOOK
Keith Lamdin and David Tilley

TOOLS FOR REFLECTIVE MINISTRY
Sally Nash and Paul Nash

TOOLS FOR
REFLECTIVE MINISTRY

SPCK Library of Ministry

SALLY NASH and PAUL NASH

First published in Great Britain in 2009

Society for Promoting Christian Knowledge
36 Causton Street
London SW1P 4ST

British Library Cataloguing-in-Publication Data
A catalogue record for this book is available from the British Library

ISBN 978–0–281–05993–5

The publisher and author acknowledge with thanks permission to
reproduce extracts from the following:
Lyrics from 'Impossibly beautiful' by Note for a Child from the album
Impossibly Beautiful, 2003 (see <www.noteforachild.com>),
used with permission.
Iona Creed © The Iona Community, from the *Iona Abbey Worship Book*,
2001, used with permission.
Extract from 'Good days bad days' by Voirrey Farrell from *Looking
Through Glass: Prayers for Healing and Wholeness*, ed. Susan Watterson,
Veritas Publications, 2006, used with permission.
Extract from 'Peter's fire' by Marie Calvert from *Looking Through Glass:
Prayers for Healing and Wholeness*, ed. Susan Watterson, Veritas
Publications, 2006, used with permission.
Extract from the poem 'Lord's Test', written by John Augustine Snow and
published in his poetry collection *Moments and Thoughts* by Kaye &
Ward Publishers in 1973.
Every effort has been made to seek permission to use copyright material
reproduced in this book. The publisher apologizes for those cases where
permission might not have been sought and, if notified, will formally
seek permission at the earliest opportunity.

1 3 5 7 9 10 8 6 4 2

Typeset by Graphicraft Limited, Hong Kong
Printed in Great Britain by Cromwell Press Group

Produced on paper from sustainable forests

This book is dedicated to
the Community of Aidan and Hilda
and the Northumbria Community,
who introduced us to the Celtic saints and values,
and who inspire and encourage
our spiritual journeys and ministry

Contents

Contents

Part II
CONTEXTS

Contents

Acknowledgements

This book is a reflection of our lives in ministry yet has its roots way before that. It is dedicated to all who have helped shape us on our journey. Sally grew up in an environment where learning and curiosity were encouraged and reflection was part of life. Paul is grateful to his mum who got him a place in college where he finally found a field where learning became a joy and a place of flourishing. We appreciate too the youth workers who invested in us and set us on our Christian journey, for Paul at Grays Baptist Church and for Sally at Wycliffe Baptist Church in Reading. Westminster Chapel nurtured an interest in theology in Paul, led him into youth work and supported him for many years as a missionary with Youth for Christ before he was ordained. Sally's passion for ministry was sparked by working with the Church Army, running a holiday club for children on Army bases in Germany when she was 17 and 21. Her journey also led her to Youth for Christ first as a volunteer and then on the staff.

We have worked with many people over the years who have inspired, encouraged and challenged us. We particularly want to thank the volunteers we worked with while running YFC programmes, students from the Midlands Centre for Youth Ministry (MCYM), members of churches where we have worshipped, especially Aston Parish Church where Paul was a curate and Sally a Reader, and where we got to try out lots of these ideas, and the staff teams we have worked with in our various jobs. We are grateful also to those we have not met but who have inspired us by their writings, songs, films and art, some of which we use in this book.

The original idea for this book originated in Paul's MA in Adult Education with Theological Reflection (with the University of Chester) and in Paul and Sally's reflections and teaching in a range of contexts. Thanks to Jo Pimlott, our colleague at MCYM, who helped us with editing, and to Rebecca Mulhearn at SPCK who had faith in our proposal for both this book and our previous publication (with Jo), *Skills for Collaborative Ministry*. Proceeds from this book support the work of the Midlands Centre for Youth Ministry.

Introduction

*We glance at our to-do list and will never find written there –
encounter mystery; be dazzled and amazed; receive a great teaching from an unexpected source.*   *(Drew Leder)*

*One day, there was a big storm. I imagine I was a bit scared as
even now I don't really like the sound of thunder. To make us feel
safer perhaps, or to try and cheer us up, my brother and I were
told the legend that there was a pot of gold to be found at the end
of a rainbow. The next morning, when the weather had cleared
up, we all went out into the garden and began digging. Buried
in the garden was a pot of gold – or a handkerchief with an S on
containing coins – which was close enough for me aged three or
four! Ever since that day, rainbows have had a special significance
for me and experiences such as this have inspired a desire to reflect
and explore the world.*   *(Sally)*

Why this book?

We are committed to the idea of lifelong learning in creative, integrated, holistic and transforming ways. We married in 1986 and
have seen each other go on many journeys as we have explored,
studied, taken on different roles and responsibilities and faced and
responded to adversity. Both of us have a Christian faith rooted in
a belief in the Trinitarian God and each of us has a passion to see
others achieve their potential, to become more Christ-like and to experience life in all its fullness (John 10.10). Being reflective helps us
in this journey. We have found in reflection a tool that helps us work
through issues to a place of peace, hope and sometimes resolution.
The problem may not be solved, the person may not have changed
but our attitude, perspective and ability to cope have.

At the Midlands Centre for Youth Ministry we have worked with
colleagues to develop an approach to reflection based on strands of
holistic learning which incorporate the personal, spiritual, professional,
ministerial, theological and academic. Inherent in this are such

1

things as ethics, leadership, relationships, work–life balance, physical and emotional dimensions. We use the tools in this book to facilitate reflection on these areas. A reflective approach to life and ministry helps us to be more integrated, to consider our life as a whole rather than as a series of compartments.

The purpose of this book is to inspire a reflective lifestyle, share some of our own ideas and those of others we find useful, and to encourage development of tools for your context. In this book there are over 150 tools, exercises and triggers for reflection. These tools can resource a wide range of ministry (and other) contexts and can be used in groups, working one to one and in personal reflection. We regularly use them in:

- pastoral care, supervision, vocation discernment, spiritual direction
- team-building and leadership teams
- work with children, young people and adults of all ages
- away days, quiet days, retreats
- education, training, preaching
- personal, professional and spiritual development
- at work, church and the other places we volunteer.

At a very basic level a question is a tool for reflection; it encourages us to think and the intention is to elicit a response. Throughout the book we ask questions to initiate reflection and encourage application of the material. In each chapter we have included short questions for reflection as well as longer 'For further reflection' boxes which include other ideas and suggestions for reflecting.

To give an example of the benefits of tools for reflection we use a Möbius strip. This is formed by taking a long strip of paper, twisting it once and joining the ends. When you trace the face of the paper you find that what was the outside has now become the inside but as you continue it becomes the outside again. The Möbius strip illustrates one of our underpinning beliefs: 'whatever is inside us continually flows outward to help form, or deform, the world – and whatever is outside us continually flows inward to help form or deform, our lives . . .' (Palmer, 2004, pp. 47–8). A reflective approach to ministry enables us to be more aware of this flow and to identify areas for growth and healing, to process issues and incidents and become more whole.

Introduction

What is reflection?

Recently watching television, we heard someone talking about propagating plants and realized that in our case we don't propagate plants, we purchase them. The two things are very different. We drew spiritual parallels with this, reflecting on which category those who have joined our church might fall into. Have they transferred in from another church or started coming through our community work or a friend? The answer to this would inevitably have an impact on the most appropriate strategy for the church.

Chapter 1 explores reflection in detail but for now we can start with Moon's contention that it is 'a form of mental processing – like a form of thinking – that we may use to fulfil a purpose or to achieve some anticipated outcome' (2004, p. 82). We would say reflection is giving something appropriate attention and consideration, looking at it from a variety of perspectives, being aware of the lenses we use, and making a response. We talk about being reflective as we see it as an attitude as much as an action. Becoming habitually reflective, which is our goal, can be a long-term endeavour requiring patience but:

> we need reminding that some things refuse to come in a hurry. Trees, gardens, the best wines, learning a language, gaining wisdom, a rewarding relationship; all these things take time and cannot be rushed. To reject patience is to miss out on some of the best things that life has to offer. (cited in Balding, 2007)

Reflection also requires effort. The Pareto Principle describes how we tend to achieve 80 per cent of our outcomes from 20 per cent of our inputs <www.businessballs.com>. As well as being a helpful tool in itself, this is often true in reflection. To go the last 20 per cent, to get the real nuggets out of an experience, often takes that extra bit of time we don't always feel we have. Paul has found this to be a significant insight which applies to many areas of his ministry, not just reflection. Conversely, there are some times in ministry when we have to work at a good-enough level because that's all that is feasible at the time. Not a happy thought for perfectionists! Using this tool to reflect on how we expend our energy in the most efficient way is vital in helping us to be good stewards of our sometimes rarest resources, time and energy.

Ministry

Ministry is about service; it is the responsibility of the whole body of Christ. Paul's personal philosophy of ministry is based upon knowing and loving himself, God and others and seeing that as an ongoing journey of service in and towards community. It involves the whole of our lives. Personal and spiritual growth are often a significant part of the early years of ministry, whether full time or as a volunteer, as we grapple with what, who and where God has called us to. Nelson suggests that in our first decade of ministerial development we need to engage with five areas:

- recognition of our own uniqueness
- identification of our limitations
- development of our leadership skills
- integration of our identity as minister
- acceleration of our spiritual formation (1988, pp. 15–23).

For our ongoing ministerial journey we would add:

- working out how to sustain ourselves for the long haul
- identifying and processing the baggage we bring
- liberating ourselves from false expectations
- developing a rule and rhythm of life that nourishes
- understanding what it means for us to keep becoming more like Christ
- working towards greater coherence between theology we profess and theology we live.

Implicit in such lists is an invitation to work out these issues for yourself, thus:

Nouwen identifies the five essential tasks of ministry as:

- teaching
- preaching
- individual pastoral care
- organizing
- celebrating (1971, p. 114).

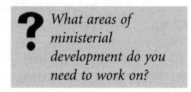
What areas of ministerial development do you need to work on?

While this may work well for a church-based setting we don't frame our particular callings in these terms. Our list is:

- facilitating learning
- encouraging
- equipping
- liberating
- healing
- empowering
- leading
- being prophetic.

? *What are your essential tasks of ministry?*

In this book, we draw from different facets of our ministry and those of others and encourage reflection on the big questions and issues as well as day-to-day life. When we look around us, our community, the people, their needs, their struggles, the world . . . what breaks our heart? What breaks God's heart? What is our response to this? We have to work out our calling in the midst of pain and, for us, reflecting processes help us to engage with and work through the related issues and experiences.

Paul has asked himself why it is important to write and share some of his insights even though, as someone with dyslexia, he finds writing hard. He concluded that one of the factors was that of legacy – being childless and wanting to leave something of himself. We have learnt to ask ourselves the difficult questions, to explore what we are fearful of, what the questions and doubts are that subtly influence our ministry. Knowing and understanding ourselves, God and others is often a multilayered process, and reflection helps us go deeper and become more self-, other- and God-aware. In ministry, who we are is more important than what we do, and developing a Christ-like character should be given at least equal weight to developing ministry skills.

? *What are the difficult questions and issues you need to reflect on currently?*

Discernment and decision-making

Testing the outcomes which emerge from reflection is good practice, helps us live within our values and beliefs, and may assist in avoiding making mistakes (Judges 21.25; 1 Thessalonians 5.21). These are our guidelines for testing the outcome of our reflection:

- Is it in harmony with our understanding of the Bible?
- Is it coherent with our values?
- Does it build the kingdom of God?
- Do I have an inner peace beyond 'if it feels good do it!'?
- Do I sense the witness of the Holy Spirit?
- Will it bring life?
- Can I do this with integrity?
- Is it in line with my personal and/or professional ethics?
- Am I willing to be accountable over this?
- Have I discussed this with others or brought it to my community? Why? Why not?

It can be helpful to write your own list, or at least have a mental checklist, to assess the outcomes of your reflections. In a question-and-answer panel with students we were once asked how we hear God. This book encourages us to listen to and encounter God in a myriad of ways but we need to discern what it is we have heard and found.

Learning and learning styles

The learning explored here is known as experiential learning, which derives from theorists such as Lewin, Dewey and Piaget and can be defined as 'the process whereby knowledge is created through the transformation of experience' (Kolb, 1993, p. 155). There are various ways this process can be described and it is often presented as some sort of learning cycle. Terms that are used include:

- concrete experience, reflective observation, abstract conceptualization and active experimentation
- problem finding, question asking, answer seeking and portrayal of knowledge
- incorporation, incubation, insight and verification (Kolb, 1993, p. 151).

We adopt a straightforward cycle that can be used in most contexts. (See Table 1.1 on p. 8.)

Reading this book you are likely to find some ideas that really resonate and others that hold little attraction. Part of the reason for this is different approaches to learning. Thinking back to something you really enjoyed learning and considering the methods used can help you identify what your preferences may be. Learning styles theory can illuminate our approach to reflection and help us when we are facilitating others. We often use Honey and Mumford's material <www.peterhoney.com> because it was developed in a British context and the learning styles are straightforward and connect well into different stages of the learning cycle as Table 1.1 illustrates.

Most of us have a stronger preference for one of these styles although we may draw on the others. If you do not already know which learning style you have and don't obviously connect to anything in Table 1.1, then search online where there are a variety of resources to help you discover more about the way you learn and reflect. Learning style theory is good to consider when reflecting with a group as it can be beneficial to have a range of activities that connect with different learning styles to enable everyone to get something out of an event. Lamdin and Tilley, in an earlier book in this series (2007), explore both learning and learning styles in the ministry context and offer additional insights.

How to make the most of reflecting

Below are some suggestions to help you make the most of reflection. Not all of the suggestions will apply to every type of reflective tool or to every context; take what you need and what suits your preferences.

General suggestions

- Create a sense of space and don't rush.
- Get comfortable, relax.
- Consider using a centring exercise (see p. 82) or focus on a lit candle or image for a short time.
- Give space for the exercise to speak for itself.
- Do not be afraid of silence.
- Be non-judgemental.
- Be gentle yet honest with yourself.
- Be aware of your go-to places and where you hesitate to go.

Table 1.1 Learning styles and stages of the learning cycle (adapted from Honey and Mumford, 1992, pp. 2–7)

Stage of the learning cycle	Learning style	Explanation
1 Having an experience	Activist	Activists enjoy new experiences, are open-minded and enthusiastic and often have a trial-and-error approach to learning. They can get bored with the longer-term implementation or with anything they regard as dull or routine. They are often gregarious and like learning activities that involve participation and challenge. Philosophy: I'll try anything once
2 Reviewing the experience	Reflector	Reflectors like to have the time and space to think about what they are doing. They may not want to contribute to discussions early on and enjoy processing their thoughts. They will often adopt a low profile in a group and enjoy times of quiet and activities where they can observe and think and are not forced to take part. Philosophy: to be cautious and consider all angles
3 Concluding from the experience	Theorist	Theorists enjoy taking what they have learnt and adapting and integrating their observations into theories. They enjoy analysis and synthesis but can struggle with out-of-the-box thinking or too much flippancy or subjectivity. They enjoy activities that challenge their thinking and will debate, discuss and often happily listen to talks or lectures. Philosophy: prize logic and rationality
4 Planning the next step	Pragmatist	Pragmatists like to take ideas, theories and techniques and see if they work in practice. They look for new ideas and enjoy experimentation. They tend to want to implement ideas swiftly and can be impatient with more measured approaches. They like taking decisions and problem-solving. They enjoy activities which seem to connect to real life or have an obvious application. Philosophy: there is always a better way and if it works it's good

Reflecting in groups

Chapter 9 is about reflecting together and contains a section on setting ground rules around such things as confidentiality, which we recommend as a starting point. Reflection can raise difficult issues in people's lives and it is important to have thought through what to do should these be disclosed. This may range from meeting for a chat, making a referral to the pastoral care team or even suggesting that the person gets professional help. If reflective activities are going to be run in a variety of groups it may be worth looking at training the leaders and explaining church or agency policies on these issues. Watts, Nye and Savage (2001) provide some helpful insights here. When reflecting in groups it is good to:

- remember people bring the history of their day with them posit-ively and negatively;
- be aware of not abusing the power you have as a facilitator – we can be much more intimidating than we think;
- remember different learning styles;
- encourage participation, even interruptions, and tell people to share or not as they choose;
- explain the exercise and ask if there are any questions.

Journalling

Insights from our reflection are worth recording. We sometimes only realize the significance of an experience or thought when we look back at it or when we see it in the broader context of what else has been going on. This is where journalling comes in. At its best journalling can be 'a tool for self-discovery, an aid to concentration, a mirror for the soul, a place to generate and capture ideas, a safety valve for the emotions, a training ground for the writer, and a good friend and confidant' (Klug, 2002, p. 7). The Bible sets a precedent for recalling what God has done for us. For example, acts of God were recited to the Israelites (Nehemiah 8.1–3) and God's dealings with humanity are central to the praise and worship of believers (Osborn, 1990, p. 13). Reading the journals of others can be inspiring and enlight-ening too. Our favourite is Nouwen's *The Genesee Diary* (1976).

If you don't already write a journal it can take some discipline and time to establish the practice. Smith encourages us not to be too hard on ourselves if we are not writing 'significant thoughts' (1992, p. 53). There are plenty of books about journal writing (some are suggested in Further reading) and these will offer specific ideas for the process. However, the most useful piece of advice is just to write! Don't worry too much about the content and initially don't analyse too much, just get your thoughts out. If prompts are helpful, Klug lists things you may wish to write about: personal events, reaction to events, conversations, prayers, questions, memories, insights, joys, gratitude, achievements, failures, world events, your reading, quotations, letters/emails/texts, travel, observations from nature, nonverbal material (2002, ch. 4). Both of us write in a journal as part of our quiet time. Sally has dated entries and prose but Paul has a book where he notes down ideas, insights, etc. with a different page per concept and he revisits and develops them. A friend illustrates her journal with pictures and sketches both of which are tools for reflection for her.

Journal writing can facilitate healing (Klug, 2002, ch. 11) and on occasion it may be that extended writing around an experience brings further insight and possibly resolution. Ensley and Herrmann explain the process:

> We have lots of mental clutter, and underneath that clutter are the images, memories and stories, and thoughts that form our spiritual core . . . Writing makes this inner world concrete. Our problems become visible. And when we see them clearly, we can then hand them over to the God who comforts and mends. (2001, p. x)

Miriam used her journal to explore feelings about the vicar leaving and in writing realized that she was trusting in her vicar rather than God, and that the focus needed to shift back to God. Blogging is a contemporary style of journal writing. Obviously it is more public than other journals would be, but people's blogs are clearly tools for reflective ministry and the benefit of their being out there is that others can learn from their reflections too.

Reviewing a journal helps get the most out of it; this can be in preparation for spiritual direction, as part of a retreat, or just a periodic reflection. It can be helpful to develop a key to mark up your journal and for this reason leaving a margin down one of the sides for later insights can be useful. If you keep your journal on a computer then there is usually a review function that enables you to add comments. Colour coding is an alternative and this makes it easy to pick out themes and patterns. You may want to highlight such things as insights, ideas, actions, issues that need further reflection, prayers, problems, dreams, hopes, prophecy and significant Bible passages.

The rest of the book

We have tried to write in a way that is accessible to people in a range of ministry contexts from cell/house group leaders, youth workers and Sunday-school teachers, to those who work in ministry settings full time and who may have had theological training. The Further reading suggestions indicate where to go to explore topics or concepts at greater depth. The book also lends itself well to developing into a course where you take a chapter a week and invite people to explore different ways of reflecting and encountering God.

In this introduction we have presented material which is a resource to get the most out of subsequent chapters. The first two chapters present foundational theory, the first on being reflective and the discipline of reflective practice and the second on theological reflection. Although we have discrete chapter headings, being reflective isn't something we can easily compartmentalize and the material from each chapter will inevitably draw on and overlap with other chapters. We see the examples of tools we have given as being illustrative rather than prescriptive and hopefully you will be inspired and challenged

> ? *What do you need to do now to get the most out of reflection?*

to develop your own tools and find your ministry enriched through the process as well as enabling others to have a more reflective approach to faith and life.

Part 1
FOUNDATIONS

1

Being reflective

Let silent contemplation be your offering.
(Anzac Memorial, Sydney)

Seeing God in the ordinary is not only about how full or empty
your calendar is, but about how attentive you're prepared to be
even if rushing around. *(Michael Frost)*

We are what we repeatedly do. Excellence, then, is not an act but
a habit. *(Aristotle)*

'Can I come and see you, please?' How do you feel when you hear
these words? Excited, because you enjoy the cut and thrust of pastoral encounters, or apprehensive because you have no idea what you
may be confronted with and whether you have the resources to deal
with it? We may begin to reflect before we see the person, speculate
perhaps as to the reasons they want to see us. As we meet with them
we are exploring best or most appropriate ways to respond, making
assessments and judgements about the other person, about ourselves. Afterwards we think about what we did, how we might have
done it better. In essence, we are engaging in reflection before, during and after the experience. This book seeks to help such reflection
become more effective as most of us don't share God's experience of
looking at all we have done and saying it was very good (Genesis 1.31)!

Setting the context

Ministry throws up all sorts of dilemmas, problems and issues that
we need to respond to. Often these responses are not straightforward
and that's where reflection comes in. It provides us with tools,
approaches and strategies that help us deal with the situation. If you
check on Amazon you will find the term 'reflection' or 'reflective' linked

with fields such as education, nursing, social work and professional development as well as ministry. The discipline of reflective practice is part of initial training and continuing professional development in these areas and is a transferable skill that we take with us wherever we go. The move to a reflective mode of learning at work is a twenty-first-century emphasis, building on a focus on organizational learning in the 1990s and on training before that. It is a response to the need to manage complexity and ambiguity (Cressey *et al.*, 2006, p. 15). Fook and Gardner (2007, p. 3) emphasize the need for critical reflection; its absence can lead to a context where practitioners feel a sense of powerlessness, fear risk, face increased complexity and work in organizations that put pressure on them to work to rules and procedures, record everything, be outcome focused and sometimes have values different from those of the agency they work for. Those of us in the caring professions may well have experienced some of this. Reflection should help us process the good, bad, disturbing, challenging and significant experiences of ministry as well as the mundane.

Schon, one of the most influential writers in the field of reflective practice, argues that people problems don't have easy solutions:

> In the varied topography of professional practice, there is a high, hard ground which overlooks a swamp. On the high ground, manageable problems lend themselves to solution through the use of research based theory and technique. In the swampy lowlands, problems are messy and confusing and incapable of technical solution.   (1983, p. 54)

This reflects the reality of ministry. However good our initial training, or despite our experience, there are almost never ready-to-use responses or solutions to our day-to-day work. This book explores some of the ways we can explore or seek solutions or explanations in the 'swampy lowlands'.

'Being reflective' is described by Moon as 'an orientation to practice or other aspects of life and it seems to imply a quality in a person who uses reflection frequently, comfortably, and – perhaps by implication – publicly, and who demonstrates that it has value for their work' (2000, pp. 158–9). She concludes that in such people reflection would

> **?** *What areas feel like 'swampy lowlands' for you?*

be habitual and that a range of forms of reflection could be easily accessed and used. For example, watching an RNLI (Lifeboats) film we heard their motto: 'Train one, save many.' At one time that would have just passed us by but now it helps us explore philosophies and priorities for ministry.

Reflecting on how we learn may help us be more effective in developing our reflection skills. We can think about an area where we are highly skilled or competent and ask ourselves, how did we get to be like that? What about an area where we feel we lack skill? What has contributed to our being like that? Did something go wrong with our learning or did we never get an opportunity to learn? What keeps us going when we don't want to learn?

> **?** *How do the answers to these questions help you in developing your skills in reflective ministry?*

In essence, being reflective involves learning from our experiences. Boud *et al.* (1993, pp. 8–16) offer a range of propositions about learning from experience that have implications for our reflection:

1 *Experience is the foundation of, and the stimulus for learning* All of our experiences can be a stimulus for learning although our disposition to learn will affect the extent to which this happens. We need to frame an experience as one we can learn from.

2 *Learners actively construct their experience* We interpret and impart meaning to what happens to us. We see things through our own eyes. One of the tasks we have to do is respond to students' comments on the modules that we teach. Inevitably we have different students making positive and negative comments about exactly the same thing – it is certainly true that you can't please everyone all of the time but you can please some of the people some of the time! This is important for us in ministry. We often have an educative agenda but what we do is framed and interpreted by students' prior experiences and who they are.

3 *Learning is a holistic experience* Learning impacts the whole of who we are and it can be difficult to distinguish between the cognitive (thinking) and the affective (feeling), for example, as in reality they can be so interlinked. Learning also happens all the time, not just on designated occasions.

4 *Learning is socially and culturally constructed* The social setting and values of our learning environment have a profound effect on the way that we learn. Sometimes our youth work students seem to minimize the effort they make and the grades that they achieve and it is almost like a repeat of school where it was not cool to be a 'swot' or admit that you did a significant amount of work to achieve your grades.

5 *Learning is influenced by the socio-emotional context in which it occurs* We all have baggage from previous learning; some of this may be positive but it can also be negative. A lot of this will involve feelings engendered by previous learning experiences, which are evoked in any new context. Acknowledging and being real about this and about how we feel within our current learning group can help us be more fully aware of what is impacting our capacity to reflect.

Win-win

This is an example of reflection from Paul drawing on some of these elements. Paul likes Covey's win-win concept (1989). Covey explains that when seeking to resolve problems with another individual there are four possible outcomes: win-lose, lose-win, lose-lose, win-win. When seen like this it is clear that win-win is the most fruitful but that's not what Paul used to do. Like many of us he was used to resolving differences by trying to persuade others that his way was best. Paul has now fundamentally changed the way he relates to people. He first seeks to hear their views, needs and hopes and to agree an outcome where at least some of these are realized. In a deeper engagement with this idea, Paul seeks to achieve harmony when making decisions. As he reflected further he realized that win-win gave him a framework to work out his natural values. It now appears obvious that win-win is the best approach but initially it was a completely new idea to Paul.

Another example of win-win in action is our allocation of household chores. When we first got married we creatively discussed who should do what. We were both in full-time ministry and busy. Sally was frustrated that Paul didn't always do things in what she perceived to be the required time frame, so she now does time-dependent things like shopping and bills and Paul does washing and ironing, which he can fit in when he likes. He usually irons when he wakes up early at the weekends but, because the shopping has been done, he always has fresh milk for the cup of tea he needs before he starts.

'Can't do', 'can do', 'do well'

This may apply to our reflection skills, but is introduced here to illustrate how concepts or ideas that we have found elsewhere can be adapted as tools for reflection. There is a saying we have both found to be true: 'Whatever you believe you *can do*, you will; and whatever you believe you *can't do*, you won't.' In our lives we have looked at the idea that you try and move your 'can't dos' to 'can dos' and 'can dos' to 'do well'.

Stage 1 Begin by identifying what skills and knowledge we need within our ministries, then place them into one of the three categories: 'can't do', 'can do', 'do well'.

Stage 2 Once we have identified what we need we should reflect on whether any of these attributes are in our 'can't do' box and if so look at developing a strategy to try and develop them (or see if such gaps are filled by others in our team).

Stage 3 Alongside this we can reflect on whether we want to move anything from 'can do' to 'do well'.

This grid can be used to grow in many areas from the simple to the complex. Mark never learnt to type and painstakingly used two fingers when he needed to produce something. He realized that he would be more effective at work if he could type proficiently so took a home teaching course. He moved a 'can't do' to a 'can do'. An example of moving something from 'can do' to 'do well' is Paul doing children's funerals. The move partly happened through experience but also by reflecting on his theology and pastoral practice to the extent that he knows what he believes and what he can say (although this evolves with ongoing reflection).

Different minds

Being reflective is one of the ways we learn to be 'ministers' (we are using this term generically to cover all types of ministry, not just church leadership). Gardner, a psychologist, has been at the forefront of exploring thinking such as multiple intelligences (Gardner, 2000). He argues that there are five ways we need to be able to think to enable coping with changes in the future, each of which offers something to being reflective:

- the disciplinary mind
- the synthesizing mind
- the creating mind
- the respectful mind
- the ethical mind (Gardner, 2006).

It is difficult to talk about a discipline of ministry and get unanimous agreement as constructs of ministry are influenced by such things as culture, theology and tradition. However, for those of us in ministry it is vital that we continue to work at our craft, see ourselves as life-long learners and remain passionate about both our work and our continuing development. These different elements proposed by Gardner help provide us with a broader context in which to place our goal to become more reflective. They also help us be aware of a wider agenda when we are designing learning events for and with other people.

Learning from their example

As we read our Bibles we see how people's actions demonstrate a capacity to be reflective or not and we can learn from their example. Martha probably regretted going and whining to Jesus about her sister (Luke 10.40); reading the text it sounds more like the sort of thing we encounter from young children than from an adult who on a different occasion recognized Jesus as the Messiah (John 11.27). Paul had clearly spent time thinking about how best to communicate to the Athenians (Acts 17.22f.) yet decided not to let John Mark travel with him, having been disappointed at his behaviour (Acts 15.37–9). If only Peter had stopped to think how to respond when the servant girl asked him if he knew Jesus (Matthew 26.69) then he wouldn't have experienced the pain of denying him. However, Jesus realized that he needed forgiveness and restoration (John 21.15f.).

? *Who do you identify with in the Bible? Does that give you an insight into how you reflect?*

Defining and exploring reflection

Continuing from our definition in the Introduction, reflection is:

> a form of mental processing – like a form of thinking – that we may use to fulfil a purpose or to achieve some anticipated outcome or we may simply 'be reflective' and then an outcome can be unexpected. Reflection is applied to relatively complicated, ill-structured ideas for which there is not an obvious solution and is largely based on the further processing of knowledge and understanding we already possess.
>
> (Moon, 2004, p. 82)

Hillier (2002, p. 7) suggests that 'when we reflect, we not only challenge our assumptions about why we do what we do, we can also help ourselves identify where we feel lacking and why we might be setting ourselves unnecessarily un-achievable standards'. For those of us who are perfectionists this latter insight can begin a journey to freedom. Johns (2004, p. 2) has a list which delineates layers of reflection beginning with 'doing reflection' and moving to 'reflection as a way of being':

- *reflection-on-experience* – reflection after the event with the intention of drawing insights to inform future practice
- *reflection-in-action* – pausing and making sense of an experience as it is going on to maybe reframe the situation to achieve desired outcomes
- *the internal supervisor* – dialogue with self while involved in a conversation with someone else
- *reflection-within-the-moment* – awareness of how we are thinking, feeling and responding to the experience and dialoguing with self to ensure that our response is congruent and having space to change your mind rather than being fixed about how to proceed
- *mindful practice* – being aware of self intending to achieve our idea of desirable practice.

It may be beneficial to reflect on where we are in this continuum and think about how we might progress to the next level if we are not yet at the stage of mindful practice.

One of the dangers of ministry is that we endlessly meet the needs of others without giving time to some of the important things

Table 1.2 Prioritizing grid

	Urgent	Non-urgent
Important	1	3
Not important	2	4

that God has called us to. Early on in our time in ministry we were introduced to the grid shown in Table 1.2 but have often failed to use it to prioritize wisely.

The essence of this model is that we need to give appropriate energy to all four areas. The general observation made is that most of us are effective at dealing with area 1, we get waylaid and give attention to 2 and 4 and therefore do not spend enough time on area 3, the important but non-urgent aspects of life and ministry. We thus may miss out on some of the dreams and larger developments we would like to achieve. We have struggled to move to mindful practice on this and perhaps have only just got there in 25 years of ministry. Email and other such media can be fantastic to deal with the urgent and important but sometimes it feels like there is an inbox of non-urgent and unimportant which takes up so much time.

We thought about this book for over six years, it was really important to each of us but was never urgent. It took an SPCK editor initiating a trip to St John's to birth it. However, we have been building towards it. One of the habits we have got into since 2004 is to have a writing week away each year and have used that to develop teaching materials, write articles or booklets. Paul enjoys these weeks so much now he wants to do two a year! Another illustration on a more personal level is with Sally and golf. She has been playing longer than Paul but has never had a handicap. She has talked about getting one for a long time but never seemed to get around to doing it until finally this summer she decided she should act. This then became an urgent task as she tends to play golf only on holiday and her final round was in the pouring rain – something she usually avoids! One of Paul's colleagues says he uses this model as a part of his 'everyweek' life and plans to do something on his important not urgent list every week to ensure he doesn't lose sight of what really is important.

Our definition of reflection in the context of ministry, drawing on both theory and our own experience, is that:

Reflection on ministry is a way of thinking about complex/multi-layered/unpredictable situations or issues and exploring possible solutions or responses, drawing on theoretical and theological understandings, cultural and self-awareness, previous experiences, intuition and the wisdom of others as appropriate, and bringing this thinking to a suitable conclusion.

Intuition

Reflection doesn't negate the use of intuition, which is quite common in ministry either in respect of something we just know or feel or the way we sometimes explain recognizing (sometimes in retrospect) the Holy Spirit guiding us in a particular context. Claxton (2003, p. 50) explains that intuition is manifested in many ways:

as emotions; as physical sensations; as impulses or attractions towards certain goals or courses of action; as images and fantasies; as faint hunches and inklings; and as aesthetic responses to situations. Intuitions are holistic interpretations of situations based on analogies drawn from a largely unconscious experiential database.

Because of the very nature of intuition it is important that material gathered from this source is the subject of reflection too as our intuition can be inspired and right, or the product of eating too much cheese for supper!

Purpose of reflection

Reflection has many purposes in ministry; it may:

- develop self-awareness;
- help us understand how we learn;
- enable us to see how we are integrating values into practice;
- help us explain what we do to our stakeholders;
- empower us as practitioners as we grow in confidence and have a better understanding of what we do;
- liberate us from some of our preconceptions or assumptions about ourselves, others or our ministry;
- help us solve problems in a creative rather than formulaic way;
- encourage us to work with metaphors and images that bring fresh insights;
- lead to action or decision;
- develop our capacity to deal with new situations as they arise.

It has helped us with things like accepting both our gifts and limitations, recognizing more of the unique contribution that we make in our contexts, developing appropriate ways of working, leading, studying, finding a rhythm of life and work that sustains us in ministry and making our relationships work! Our aim through our work is to develop reflective practitioners and it is always encouraging to get an email or have a conversation where people talk about often drawing on what they learnt at college in their new context.

For further reflection

Use the following questions or statements to trigger your own reflection:

- What causes you the greatest fear and how constructively do you deal with it?
- Just because you can, should you?
- Why are you doing this?
- For whose benefit are you doing this?
- If it is all there is, thirsty people will drink dirty water and very thirsty people will drink very dirty water.

Reflexivity

Any time we engage in reflection we bring who we are to it; there is no such thing as value-free or impartial reflection. Reflexivity is the technical term that covers the self-awareness and analysis needed. Reflexivity involves an ability to recognize:

- that all aspects of ourselves and our context influence the way we create knowledge and the knowledge we create;
- that our knowledge creation is influenced by our physicality and material contexts; our social and historical contexts; interaction; and the tools we use to create knowledge;
- how our assumptions, especially about the nature of knowledge and how it is and should be created, have an influence on the actual knowledge we create and believe in (Fook and Gardner, 2007, p. 71).

It is important to remember this when working with others who may create knowledge in a different way from us and when embarking on any new project or collaboration. An open and honest discussion about terms, concepts, ways of working and so on can avoid misunderstanding later down the line when we find out we are using words in different ways. A favourite of ours is 'now'; we have a 'Sally now' which is immediately and a 'Paul now' which is when it seems right in the midst of other things that he is involved in. We tend to clarify which 'now' we mean! Two people reflecting on the same thing may well come up with different outcomes.

Environments that facilitate reflection

Reflection is easier when our environment facilitates it. Essential elements are time and space, something that often seems in short supply in ministry. Some people find it easier to reflect while out walking which could be a doubly effective way of building in reflective time. However, it may be best to walk where you and your thoughts can be undisturbed rather than where you meet someone you know every few minutes.

Having reflection time scheduled personally or with the staff team can appear a luxury but can enhance ministerial effectiveness as learning from experience is integrated into practice. When reflection is seen as a core activity then it is more likely to occur. However, for this time to be used effectively in a team context it needs an emotionally supportive environment. This includes:

- a place where learners feel safe to take risks in their reflection;
- a good learning environment socially;
- an environment where emotional processes attached to reflection are understood and supported;
- being supportive of those who find reflection alien or difficult (Moon, 2000, p. 169).

In essence, we need to create a safe place for reflection to take place and to be willing to be supportive and understanding, ensuring that we give proper time and attention to the task.

There are also environments which hamper reflection; these might be a culture of silence where we are not encouraged to talk about what goes on, a rigid individualism where we prefer to do things on our own and don't value a more collegiate approach and a culture of secrecy because of the fear of what happens when we self-disclose (Brookfield, 1995, pp. 247–51).

It emerged in a reflection time with her boss that Julie was profoundly affected emotionally by the situation of one of the people she had been pastorally visiting. When this turned into a suggestion of being unable to maintain professional boundaries in supervision Julie felt that her boss didn't understand her approach to ministry or the purposes of reflection.

Without a shared understanding of the purposes and ground rules around reflection times they may never be used as effectively as they might, or may be prey to the 'once bitten twice shy' experience and turn into academic exercises. What we should also avoid is having a hidden agenda, or the temptation to use unethically, or inappropriately, material that emerges when someone is being vulnerable in a time of reflection.

> **?** *Can you adapt your environment to make it more reflection friendly?*

Writing to reflect

One of the ways to reflect is through writing and in the Introduction we advocated journal writing. Our students need to write reflective journals as part of assessed practice and it is encouraging to hear how, although they seem to find it difficult to get to grips with this practice at the beginning, they eventually find that it is beneficial for learning and that it helps process many of the mixed emotions and thoughts that come with ministry. Rolfe *et al.* (2001, p. 52) suggest four reasons why writing is useful.

- It is a purposeful activity that helps us focus on an issue, promotes critical thinking and helps us interact with the material of practice.
- Writing helps us order our thoughts, identify priorities, sift what is important from what is not and develop understanding through our analysis of a situation.
- Writing provides a permanent record. It helps us to recall the important elements of an experience, provides material to go back to, gives

space to contemplate and in revisiting the experience we can see how our perspective has changed over time.

- Writing helps us make connections between ideas. It helps us integrate different pieces of information; it can give a more holistic picture; it can bring insight; it can help us to gain a different perspective and determine action.

Although writing specifically about learning journals, Moon (2000, pp. 188–93) would add that writing:

- helps us explore the self, personal constructs of meaning and worldview;
- can be therapeutic or supportive of behaviour change;
- enhances creativity by making better use of intuitive understanding;
- provides an alternative 'voice' for those not good at expressing themselves verbally.

One way we might want to reflect on our ministry is to write regularly, and different ways of doing this will be explored later in the book.

Reflective practice

Reflective practice is the term used by professionals to describe the discipline we have been talking about. Johns argues that it is a holistic form of practice because it:

- focuses on the whole experience and then seeks to understand its significance within the whole;
- is grounded in the meanings the individual practitioner gives to the particular experience and seeks to facilitate such understanding;
- acknowledges that the practitioner is ultimately self-determining and responsible for his or her own destiny and seeks to facilitate such growth (2004, p. xiii).

Various definitions of reflective practice can be found in the literature, each with their own nuances; there is no uniform agreement. Thompson suggests that reflective practice is 'an approach to professional practice that emphasizes the need for practitioners to avoid standardised, formula responses to the situations they encounter' (1996, p. 221), which resonates with what we have been saying so far about being reflective. Fook and Gardner's understanding of reflective practice is that it is 'an approach designed to assist professionals to become aware of the "theory" or assumptions involved in their practice, with the purpose of closing the gap between what is espoused and what is enacted' (2007, p. 24). This understanding seems pertinent to those in ministry. Many of us will have felt the tension between our practice and what we believe it should be or the values and vision that we initially had on entering ministry. Reflective practice can help us to understand how and why we have moved.

To enable us to develop our skills in reflective practice there are a variety of things that we can do:

- Read about subjects that relate to our work to broaden our perspective and bring insight.
- Ask others about why they work in the way that they do in the hope of developing a mutually supportive atmosphere for reflective practice.
- Watch what others do and learn from our observations.
- Pay attention to feelings and try to see how they relate to our practice.
- Be willing to talk and share to facilitate learning from one another.
- Make sure thinking time is part of our regular work pattern (adapted from Thompson 1996, pp. 225–7).

Further ideas for reflection are to be found throughout this book but below are some basic models for reflecting for those who appreciate frameworks.

Ways into reflecting on practice

These ways in are offered as frameworks for reflective practice. Other chapters include a range of alternative methodologies. It is worth noting that to use any framework in a formulaic way means that there is more of a focus on completing a task and ticking it off the list rather than being genuinely reflective. We include our own models as well as those found in the literature. The latter may be beneficial when doing multidisciplinary work when you can look for a mutually agreeable starting point.

Short formulae

There are various short formulae that can be used to aid reflection. Having at the tip of our fingers a short set of questions to aid reflective practice can be useful when we encounter a situation or issue that merits reflection.

- Observe, assess, respond (this is explored further on pp. 46–7).
- What? So What? Now What? (See Rolfe *et al.*, 2001, p. 35.)
- Describe . . . what do I do?
  Inform . . . what does this mean?
  Confront . . . how did I come to be like this?
  Reconstruct . . . how might I do things differently? (See Smyth, 1996, p. 50.)
- DATA:
  *D*escribe the problem
  *A*nalyse the nature of it
  *T*heorize alternative ways to solve it
  *A*ct on basis of theory (see Peters cited by Hillier, 2002, p. 5).

Basic reflective practice model

1 *Name* What is the situation/issue/dilemma/problem/question you want to reflect on?
2 *Explore* What are you hoping will emerge from this reflective practice process? What is the end result/product/consequence . . . that you are looking for?
3 *Analyse* What is/could be going on? How do you/others think/feel? Have you made assumptions about the situation? How do my values/motives/goals/tradition/discipline influence my analysis? Do I have previous experience that helps here?
4 *Evaluate* What options or possibilities do I have? What are the benefits and drawbacks of these? What would I change/do differently? What influenced me in this situation?
5 *Outcome* What is the outcome of this process? Have I learnt something? Changed my practice? Done something?

Ministry reflection framework

First choose a situation or experience that you want to reflect on and then answer any or all of these questions as they seem relevant or appropriate. It can be helpful to write a short summary of the experience first, either in text or a mind map (for more on mind maps, see Buzan, 2005).

Self-awareness

- Why have you chosen this experience?
- What feelings are associated with this experience? Do you need to process any of these feelings on your own, in supervision or with someone else?
- What brought you life in this experience?
- What brought you death in this experience?
- Have you learnt anything about yourself through reflecting on this?
- Is there anything you need to reflect on further?

Practice

- What is the broader context of this practice experience?
- What was your role?
- What did you do?
- What did others do?
- Were your actions appropriate, ethical and effective?
- What could have been done differently or better?
- What were the consequences?
- Is there any follow-up that needs to be done?
- Is there any theory or prior learning that you can bring to this experience?
- What theological insights can you bring to this?
- What have you learnt from this?

Gibbs' reflective cycle (cited in Johns, 2004, p. 17)

- Description – what happened?
- Feelings – what were you thinking and feeling?
- Evaluation – what was good and bad about the experiences?
- Analysis – what sense can you make of the situation?
- Conclusion – what else could you have done?
- Action plan – if it arose again what would you do?

Brookfield's critical reflection lenses (Brookfield, 1995, p. xiii)

View your practice through four reflective lenses. Thus you see yourself through the eyes of:

- Lens 1 Yourself as minister – autobiographical
- Lens 2 Those you minister to
- Lens 3 Colleagues
- Lens 4 Literature, theory (and theology if using this framework for theological reflection – many can be used for both).

Johns' framing perspectives (Johns, 2004, p. 33)

For each perspective ask yourself: 'How has this experience enabled you to . . . ?'

- Philosophical – confront and clarify your beliefs and values that constitute desirable practice.
- Role – clarify your role boundaries and authority within role, and your power relationships with others.
- Theoretical – link theory with practice in meaningful ways.
- Reality perspective – appreciate and shift those forces that constrain your realization of desirable practice (embodiment, tradition and power).
- Problem – focus problem identification and resolution within the experience.
- Temporal – draw patterns with past experiences while anticipating how you might respond with appropriate skilful and ethical action in future.
- Developmental – develop your expertise using valid and appropriate frameworks.

Example of reflective practice

Jack was faced with a difficult situation as a young curate and later wrote up the experience so he could benefit from the learning. It is written in the first person, which is the most effective approach for reflective writing:

Event

A man in his late twenties knocked at the door of the church. He looked rather dishevelled and I suspected he wanted money. I opened the door with my answer ready. He asked if we needed any windows cleaning. I was taken aback and took some time to answer. I said I did not think so, but he asked again, explaining that he needed to earn a little money. His appearance did not fill me with confidence as he looked half-stoned.

The question in my mind was, 'Should I give him work?' My reservation came from a suspicion that the money would be spent on drugs. I did let him clean the windows, we agreed a price and I was pleased with the work afterwards.

Reflection

I realized I was a little uncomfortable with the encounter and sought to work out why. Why did I allow him to clean the windows and give him money? I reflected that I would not just *give* him money (it was the policy of the church to buy food, utility tokens, etc. rather than give cash which could be spent on drugs) but why was this different? The no-cash policy also meant I couldn't have *asked* him to clean windows. So was it because I thought he was at least trying to earn money rather than asking for a handout? Or did I just take the easy way out to avoid confrontation? I was still uncomfortable after these reflections as I remained unsure of my motives. Some of this was around me being judgemental. He was honest that he was trying to make a go of life and get started in window cleaning but my previous experience was of other people asking for money and feeling conned by stories I was told. He may not have been into drugs at all, I could have misinterpreted him. Judging and prejudice were at the heart of my attitude and reactions. As I thought more about what was going on I realized these questions connected into the issue in my ethical values of how I spend my money. Am I aware where the money goes for all the clothes and food I purchase or services I pay for? Or is it that the less distance I feel between me and the potential abuse the more responsible I feel for my actions? Should I have paid him and expected him to be an autonomous adult or should I have taken more care of where I spent the rest of my money? Or should I have done both?

This is a good example of reflecting before an event (the church had set a policy of not giving cash), during an event (changing an initial response as the situation developed) and after (questioning and thinking about assumptions regarding responsible spending).

Principles for reflective practice

- Value our experience.
- Take time and create space for reflection.
- Be honest with ourselves.
- Be thorough in our analysis of the situation, emotion, reaction, etc.

- Draw upon as many disciplines as possible to help make sense of the experience.
- Be aware of our blind spots, personal baggage.
- Be habitual.
- Seek to become instinctively reflective.
- Reflect before, during and after experiences.
- Always, always, always have an outcome, even if it is only temporary. Don't let your reflection remain merely a theoretical process. Something should be different as a consequence of reflecting.

Benefits of reflective practice

- Provides a simple structure to process our everyday experiences.
- Helps us access prior learning.
- Encourages application of transferable skills.
- Helps and facilitates us in dealing with things that trouble us.
- Takes learning out of the classroom and academic structures into the everyday lives of those we seek to serve.

? *What are the strengths, weaknesses, opportunities and threats (SWOT) for you around reflective practice?*

2

Being theologically reflective

Adapt yourselves no longer to the pattern of this present world, but let your minds be remade and your whole nature thus transformed. (*Romans 12.2, New English Bible*)

A theology which has no practical consequences is worth nothing at all. (*Rupert E. Davies*)

Theological reflection is about the engagement between the God we bring and the God we find in an 'experience' without being prescriptive of the outcome. (*Paul Nash*)

Theological reflection changes lives. (*Patricia Killen and John de Beer*)

Most of us ponder from time to time on the big questions of life such as, 'Who am I?' 'Why am I here?' 'What's wrong with the world?' 'What solutions are there?' The answers to such questions are often theological. Killen and de Beer write:

> As human beings we reflect, ask *why* about our lives, because we are drawn to seek meaning. We need meaning as much as we need food and drink. Our reflection is rooted in this human drive to understand, to make the truest and richest meaning possible of our lives.
>
> (1999, p. x)

As Christians it is natural to want to bring our faith into that reflection. This will shape our values, the way we live and the way we minister. Ballard and Pritchard suggest that 'Christian people are always thinking theologically, whether in rudimentary or sophisticated ways; their discussion will always betray a theological stance' (1996, p. 118). A simple example is that of how we view humanity – intrinsically good or fallen and evil? How we answer that question will be part of our framework of ministry and cannot help but shape our attitude and approach towards people.

The origins of theological reflection are well documented (e.g. Kinast, 1996; de Bary, 2003; Paver, 2006) and will not be revisited here; we focus on the whys and hows of being theologically reflective. However, we note that there has been a journey in ministerial training from talking about applied theology to theological reflection along with a discourse based on process (see Graham *et al.*, 2005) as well as an emphasis on doing theology contextually (see Bergmann, 2003; Bevans, 2002). Theological reflection is often seen as an element of practical theology.

Liberation theology has highlighted that theology can be the task of the many rather than the few. Cochrane observes that 'Ordinary believers, in their original experiences of faith and their practical reflection on daily life, however unsophisticated or flawed their theology, confront us with issues and challenges too seldom incorporated into the formal theological work of the Christian community' (1999, p. xvii). One of our aims in writing this book is to offer tools that make the task of doing theology more accessible to those 'ordinary believers' who help us understand who we are as ministers and shape our understanding of the Church, mission, ministry and leadership.

More specifically, there are at least five aspects of ministry where theological reflection is significant:

- engaging with the pastoral needs of people;
- helping to sustain the community of faith;
- finding meaning and transcendence;
- energizing the apologetic role;
- providing a corrective when necessary (de Bary, 2003, p. 41).

We wish we had been introduced to theological reflection as a tool when we first entered ministry as it might have speeded up some of our learning!

What is theological reflection?

Theological reflection is a term that means different things to people. Classically, theological reflection starts with experience and brings theology to bear on it. Paver elaborates, 'The lived experience of one's life is shaped by personal and community relationships, religious tradition, culture, politics, work, leisure time and all the multiplicity of feelings and thoughts that go to make the very fabric of a human being' (2006, p. 25). Kinast notes that the process involves our recognizing God's role in our ministry with the result that change may occur such as enhanced self-awareness, a different outlook, renewed motivation or a decision made which can lead to new action(s) (1996, pp. ii–ix). The definition we most often use is this:

> Theological reflection is the discipline of exploring individual and corporate experience in conversation with the wisdom of a religious heritage. The conversation is a genuine dialogue that seeks to hear from our own beliefs, actions, and perspectives, as well as those of the tradition. It respects the integrity of both. Theological reflection therefore may confirm, challenge, clarify and expand how we understand our own experience and how we understand the religious tradition. The outcome is new truth and meaning for living.
>
> (Killen and de Beer, 1999, p. viii)

For many people their approach to doing theology is to apply their faith to experience. This is where theological reflection can be a different, even a revolutionary way of doing theology. Theological reflection seeks to discover the God, the kingdom, the expressions of faith within the experience as opposed to having a predetermined theology which we seek to apply to the experience. In looking at various definitions and drawing on our own practice we suggest that being theologically reflective involves:

- identifying experiences that merit reflection;
- asking where God is in this situation or experience and realizing that there may be differences between the God we bring to it and the God we find who is there already;
- making connections with Christian tradition, theology and the Bible – what within my faith helps me make sense of this experience?
- making connections with our faith, our context and culture, and our experiences of ministry;
- taking action or moving on from where we started;
- integrating the new knowledge into practice, attitudes, frames of reference, etc.

Theological reflection leads us primarily to ask two questions:

1 What within my faith resources helps me make sense of, critique, go deeper into, look differently at, be enlightened by or engaged with, this situation?
2 What of God and the kingdom can be found in the experience?

It is a faith expression of reflective practice.

For further reflection

Use the following questions, images or statements to trigger your own reflection:

- Why is it harder to carry a candle while moving quickly?
- Do you really want to love the person you hate?
- Seeing a child being shouted at in a supermarket.
- Einstein's definition of stupidity: doing something over and over again and expecting different results.
- There is an illness which means you feel no pain.

Revisiting reflective practice – win-win plus theology

One of the simple definitions of theological reflection is to add faith to the reflection resources we have. So what within our faith could bring further clarity on win-win? What jumped out to Paul was a Trinitarian insight: that the different persons of the Trinity do not play win-lose. They only seek the best for each other; they are not in competition or seeking to get the better of each other. This understanding of the Trinity brings enlightenment to our experience, and the idea of win-win adds to our understanding of Trinity. Theological reflection is a two-way process; the experience influences our understanding of faith and our faith is transformed because of the experience. The final aspect is to have an outcome, to ask what will be different, what have we learnt, what will we do differently next time? In this reflection the outcome for Paul is twofold:

- It deepens his understanding of how the Trinity relates in a non-competitive manner and seeks the best for each other.
- When next in a potential conflict situation seek to understand what the other person's needs are but don't roll over for the sake of harmony.

Issues around theological reflection as a methodology

Despite the quotation at the start of the chapter ('Theological reflection changes lives') or perhaps because of it, theological reflection is not without its dangers. Our experience is that asking 'why?' is sometimes seen by others as threatening, particularly where an 'if it works do it' mentality prevails. We understand how you get to the stage of stopping asking questions because it has been easier to go with the flow than be labelled as rebellious or awkward. This can be particularly true within some church traditions where theological reflection is not necessarily encouraged as there is a 'party line' to be followed or a suspicion of any thinking that doesn't first start with 'What does the Bible say?' There are some risks in an approach that may lead us to think that experience is more important than what the Bible or other sources say, as we can all be prone to self-deception and make choices for our own benefit rather than for the wider good. Here our theological tradition will be significant because of the implications it has for how we understand the Bible. As people who grew up in the evangelical tradition it took a while for us to reflect theologically and not feel that we were being disloyal to our heritage.

Outcomes of theological reflection partly depend on the inputs, and an issue for some is a lack of knowledge of our Christian heritage, which means that what is drawn on can be quite limited. Knowledge of church history or doctrine may be found in those who have experienced ministerial training but many people in our churches will not have been exposed to teaching on such topics. Our experience of people using the Bible for reflection is that some stories are used more than others and that the Gospels are referred to more frequently than any other part of the Bible. There is a danger that theological reflection can degenerate into a simplistic version of 'what would Jesus do?' As well as engaging with our faith heritage, our experience needs to be understood in its context, which often means also drawing on social science disciplines for insight. How we resource theological reflection then becomes an issue, as we need to help people identify and engage with sources that will enable the process to be beneficial and enlightening.

Some are concerned that theological reflection is often taught in a way that is disconnected from other theological endeavour. Graham *et al.* speculate on what would happen if theological reflection were seen as fundamental to the development of Christian thought. This, they suggest, could lead to theology being seen as a 'practical wisdom' or a way of living wisely and that God talk may emerge from experiencing and questioning everyday life (2005, p. 8). There is a necessity for us to understand our own worldview and see how we can sometimes impose this on our reading of the Bible or other texts. Ballard and Pritchard raise concerns over certain models of theological reflection where Christians ask for insights

> **?** *Do you have any issues about theological reflection as a methodology that you need to acknowledge and work through?*

from religious texts and the level of simple authority that can be unhelpfully given to such methods:

> In an extreme form this approach may even implicitly locate God in a book, a church or a lecture room and disregard the conviction of faith that God will be found already at work in the ambiguities and struggles of the modern world. (1996, p. 121)

Skills and qualities needed for theological reflection

To be theologically reflective we need to watch, look, look again, listen, ask questions, have an ability to judge, discern, apply wisdom and identify the consequences of our conclusions. One of the skills of theological reflection is to get the right balance between the danger of being certain and the discipline of exploration. Sometimes we don't pay attention to something because we think we know what to do or think in a situation, yet if we explored it through theological reflection something new might emerge. Yet it is unhelpful if we are so uncertain and insecure that we never feel we are doing something right. Being able to engage with ambiguity can be helpful but it is difficult and can be threatening. Some people would have problems with this because they have grown up (in their faith) with the need for certitude and self-assurance expressed as positive qualities. Theological reflection may appear almost frightening as we have to let go of (or at least loosen) some deeply held beliefs in the pursuit of working out what we actually think rather than just taking on board what we have inherited. Coupled with this, the postmodern context we are working in can suggest that absolute truth is arrogant and potentially oppressive, both qualities that good ministers would seek to avoid. A further skill is to be able to live with the uncertainty that is there at the beginning of the process and also the potential vulnerability as we do not know where our journey will lead us. Another of the abilities needed is not so much a skill, but more of a discipline, that of making theological reflection part of everyday life, a thought pattern that is utilized in an organized, focused way.

A willingness to be open and to share is helpful in being theologically reflective. The assertion that thorough, insightful theological reflection will not be done alone is found in much of the literature (e.g. Ballard and Pritchard, 1996; Killen and de Beer, 1999; Kinast, 1996; Whitehead and Whitehead, 1995). This will often require skilled facilitation and a commitment to helping people understand the process and equipping them with the resources to engage holistically and effectively. A difficulty for some is the accessibility of a group to reflect with. Some of the occasions of ministry that we want to reflect on may be sensitive or confidential and are perhaps best left to be explored with a mentor, a peer support group, in non-managerial supervision or perhaps with a spiritual director. If you are part of a team then having theological reflection on the agenda can be a valuable use of time and inculcate a reflective approach to ministry.

One of the difficulties faced when looking at theological reflection is that it can be seen as yet another task to add to a busy ministerial day. It is not something that should be rushed. Killen and de Beer note that:

> It takes time to do theological reflection. Such an artful practice requires learning and refining until it seeps into our being. A disciplined reflective habit of mind and heart must penetrate our being so that it becomes part of our identity and action.   (1999, p. 76)

An assessment of whether we are theologically reflective practitioners is that the discipline becomes habitual and rigorous.

Metaphors of theological reflection

There are many metaphors we find helpful in developing our thinking about theological reflection but two favourites are 'wells' and 'voices'. Paul particularly likes wells to describe the resources we access to help us engage with our experiences and we discuss this in the next chapter.

The metaphor of 'voices' illuminates our understanding and practice of reflecting generally. In taking the idea of voices seriously we need to listen to all the different people in the process, a conversation between many participants. It brings to mind the phrases we heard as children such as 'listen when I am talking to you' or 'don't interrupt, adults are talking'. We need to be aware of what messages we hear regarding theological reflection. An anti metaphor for a reflective lifestyle might be 'just do it'.

Trialogue

Dialogue is a frequently used word to describe two voices interacting together. For a theologically reflective practice and lifestyle two voices are not enough. That's why we use the word trialogue. It describes the necessity to access and listen to at least three voices in the reflective conversation. So what are these voices?

1 the voice of God and our Christian heritage
2 our own beliefs, personal and professional values and theory from our discipline
3 experience.

Any two of these are not enough to be effective theological reflectors. We leave out any one of them at our peril. We need to listen intensely to all three separately and in conversation with each other. The excitement of theological reflection is that the voices merge, blend and speak all at once. We then have to sift and give weight to the various voices as we work towards an outcome. We think this is why theological reflection is sometimes confusing. There are many thoughts happening simultaneously – our values, a piece of management theory, a Gospel passage and so on. A key question that needs to be asked is whose and which voice is always:

• listened to?
• ignored?
• spoken over?
• shouting?
• silent?

Our particular perspective is the need to listen not only to our internal ignored voices but also to those external voices who may be marginalized or unseen by society or the Christian community. We advocate listening to the voices of children and young people as they are a part of the Church that is sometimes not heard. The discipline and skill not to seek to interpret too quickly will stand us in good stead as reflectors with integrity.

Ways into theologically reflective practice

To make best use of the rest of the book we have identified a range of tools which may help in our quest to be reflective ministers. They reflect the breadth of models that are around and are drawn from different educational and ministerial contexts. Although they are presented in a linear way, as long as we are aware of the broad framework it is possible to dip in and out of them and to make connections in a more intuitive way.

The dice game

Paul has devised a game to teach theological reflection or to use as a regular feature in, for example, a staff meeting. He uses three dice to represent three stages of reflection and for each stage there are various possibilities (see Table 2.1). An individual rolls the dice at each stage and has to reflect based on the things on the sheet. This helps develop flexibility and a creative approach to reflection and can be adapted for different contexts. The numbers relate to the dice. Thus if you throw 1, 2 and 5 you are reflecting on a conversation, drawing insights from a parable and identifying a change of practice!

Although this model may seem prescriptive and limiting, we have found it beneficial as it makes theological reflection accessible even for those encountering it for the first time and the game dimension helps it seem fun. It enables people to realize the breadth of Christian resources that are available in helping us make sense of an experience. As well as the resources in the grid we can also use contextual theologies, such as liberation, feminist, black, green, and theological themes and their sub themes, such as salvation, creation, Christology, Trinity, eschatology, mission, ecclesiology and church history.

Table 2.1 Using the dice game to aid theological reflection

Dice for experience/ trigger, e.g.	Your example	Dice for faith resource, e.g.	Dice for outcome, e.g.
1 Conversation	e.g. when Raj invited me to go to the gudwara with him	1 Story about Jesus	1 New learning
2 Conflict situation		2 Parable	2 Changed behaviour
3 Film clip		3 Old Testament story	3 Fresh insight
4 Observation from nature	Waking up and seeing everything covered with snow	4 Christian heritage	4 New direction
5 Childhood memory		5 Biblical/ theological theme	5 Change of practice
6 Everyday activity		6 Image or metaphor	6 Action

Basic model

The shape of a circle has frequently been used to describe the theological reflection process. On reflection a circle does not totally fulfil the task as it looks as though it takes us back to the same place. However, a spiral is much more helpful as it expresses the ongoing nature of the reflection process (see Figure 2.1 on p. 44). We never end up back at the same place and it highlights the end of the process as always being a new place of learning or discovery.

Whitehead and Whitehead's ministry model

This model has three stages and has been developed for a ministry context with a concern for something that is portable (into daily life), performable (resulting in action) and communal. It draws on three sources: our (individual and community) experience, the religious tradition and the surrounding culture.

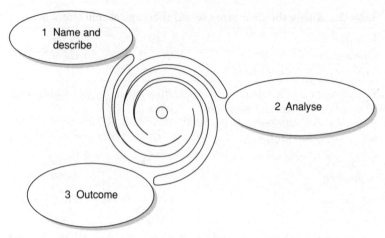

Figure 2.1 Theological reflection spiral

Stage 1   *Attending* This involves seeking out information about a specific issue or concern that can be drawn from our experience, the Christian tradition and cultural resources. It is important to listen critically but suspend judgement at this stage.

Stage 2   *Assertion* Here we gather the perspectives from the different sources and engage in a dialogue as we try to clarify our insights. For this to work effectively it is important to be open to challenge and to have courage to share our convictions.

Stage 3   *Pastoral response* Having discussed and gained insight on our issue or concern we now need to move to decision and action. This involves discerning the best way to respond, planning our response and evaluating what we have done (adapted from Whitehead and Whitehead, 1995, pp. 3–19).

Green's pastoral spiral

Green acknowledges that his spiral is very similar to the pastoral cycle developed in Latin America by liberation theologians. We have chosen this version because it has been used successfully in our context (the model was developed in the urban deanery where we live and worship).

Stage 1   *Experience* We first need to identify an event, situation, prob-
           lem or issue that causes us concern or interest. We should
           describe the experience and the feelings that are attached
           to it.

Stage 2   *Exploration* Here the key is asking the right questions, per-
           haps considering sociology and psychology, for example, as
           well as theology, and seeking to put the experience into a
           broader context.

Stage 3   *Reflection* In this phase we explore how the Christian faith
           relates to the experience, which may involve such things
           as the Bible, prayer, songs, creeds, theology and current
           teaching.

Stage 4   *Response* We need to do more than reflect. We need
           to be able to answer the question: 'In the light of all the
           experience, exploration and reflection, what does God
           now require of us?' Finally, we implement our response in
           whatever form seems most appropriate.

Stage 5   *New situation* And the spiral can begin again. As a result of
           following through on our pastoral spiral we are not in the
           position we were in when we started and we can begin
           again with a different experience (adapted from Green,
           1990, pp. 14–41).

This last point is important to us and Paul uses a children's toy
commonly known as a 'slinky' to demonstrate this when teaching
theological reflection.

Paver's transcendental model

Paver suggests that this model works when we are open and vulnerable with a willingness to engage with the influences that impact
us and our context. It is an approach that seeks integration and integrity
in our lives.

- *Starting point* is the authentic self shaped by: history, context,
  parents, cultural heritage, religious experience, education and
  socialization.
- *Conversation partners* are drawn from our relationships, experiences,
  faith influences and aspects of ourselves that affect our actions.
- *Filtered* through our tendency to self-deception, which may
  involve claiming too much or too little about ourselves and our

capabilities or disavowal or denial of some of our characteristics that we find hard to accept or engage with.

• *Leading to* new horizons and/or new action.

The strengths of this approach are the way it begins with our inner experience and takes seriously our spiritual life. The limitations are that to be most effective it requires us to be self-aware and there is always a danger in being too subjective (adapted from Paver, 2006, pp. 78–9).

Nash's observe, assess, respond model

This is a simple, three-stage process Paul developed from the classic see, judge, act model. This resulted from a piece of reflective practice in realizing that the word 'judge' is interpreted negatively by many, particularly in a youth work context. It also adds a range of resources or perspectives that we can reflect on or from. At each stage we choose various words to work with that resonate with us and identify which contexts or elements we need to consider.

Stage 1 *Observe* At this stage we are exploring our chosen experience.

Purpose and key words: Detect, investigate, insight, imagine, scrutinize, perceive, examine, witness, explore, discover, probe, glimpse, discriminate, discern, become aware of . . .

Consider: situation, dynamics, agendas, expectations, fears, hopes, human development, group theory, pressures, personality, gender, ethnicity, class, disability, culture, state of mind, health education, atmosphere, environment, weather, motives . . .

Stage 2 *Assess* Here we have a conversation between our experience and ministerial and theological resources and work to a conclusion.

Purpose and key words: Mediate, arbitrate, adjudicate, critique, decide, judge, conclude, ascertain, determine, consider, pronounce, realize, review, evaluate . . .

Consider: past experience, church tradition, theology, Bible, metaphors, theory, power, history, ministerial principles, professionalism, social and political context, culture, subculture . . .

Stage 3   *Respond* In the light of the conclusions of the previous stages, what will we change or do differently next time?
Purpose and key words: do something, proceed, be active, act, react, change; take action, start, move towards, learn, initiate, develop, begin, instigate, initiate, plan, think differently . . .
Consider: restrictions, expectations, hopes, need, resources, desires, short/medium/long-term plans, vision, reactions, consequences . . . (adapted from Nash, 2007, pp. 15–21).

Theologically reflective shopping

Our students meet in small groups and one activity we do is to meet in IKEA and give the students a notional budget (say £5–10) and ask them to find items that they could use for theological reflection. We meet in the café and people share their insights and reflections from what they found; some then choose to buy the items and use them in their contexts. An alternative is to ask everyone to visit their local pound shop and buy one thing that could be used for theological reflection and to bring it to a meeting and share it. This helps develop reflection on God in the everyday.

Being theologically reflective – examples from practice

This is an example of how we facilitate theological reflection but also engage in reflective practice ourselves in the process. The context is a student on a church placement running a fixed-term girls' group looking at self-esteem using a course without Christian content. The group was run according to good youth work practice around being educative, empowering, participative and committed to equal opportunities, but this was interpreted to mean that faith was not mentioned or integrated into any teaching. The only opportunity to share from a Christian perspective was if asked a direct question by a young person. As her tutor, Paul encouraged the student to think through this approach to youth work and whether she thought it was appropriate and what some of the key issues were. In reflecting on his practice Paul used Evans' (1999, p. 75) version of a critical incident analysis and this is his recording of it:

- *Description* The incident that provoked the reflection was the student sensing a dichotomy between the approaches to youth work in her church and in this other placement. Over the course the student had grown in an understanding of shalom as meaning a holistic understanding of salvation that is concerned with all areas of a young person's life. In dialogue we drew out her concern that it seemed incongruous to look at the topic of self-esteem with a youth group run by a church and not to at least look at the idea of our being made in the image of God. How could the course be holistic if it did not cover such a fundamental belief?

- *Analysis* The incident was critical because it challenged the student's understanding of what was 'good youth work practice' in a church context. It was critical from my perspective because it showed the student being willing and able to critique the work of practitioners who were more experienced than she was and to believe that she could have a valid different viewpoint. For me there was an element of shalom for the student in drawing closer to the qualities needed in a professionally qualified worker. She was able to see that she held an equally coherent position on what was good and appropriate practice in this context. The next stage was to encourage an appropriate response, which in her context was to journal her thoughts and argument. She also decided to raise the issue with the worker in charge of the group, which also showed professional development and growth.

- *Evaluating* A difficulty for me was that I knew the church and workers concerned outside of my role as a CYM tutor and needed to be careful not to bring in any preconceived ideas or assumptions from this knowledge and experience. I don't think I biased her conclusions. In general I tried to raise questions and affirm the student's right to hold her own opinion that was different from the one held by other leaders. I believe I empowered her over this situation.

- *Feeling* Although I felt a little awkward because of a slight blurring of boundaries, I felt very satisfied at what the student produced out of our conversations and her further reflections. It was some of her best work and showed a level of analysis I had rarely seen before in her work.

- *Synthesis* If we had worked solely in the realms of reflecting on practice without introducing a theological element then the work within the youth group would have been perceived as very good and contributing towards the welfare of young people concerned. However, a key element was missing, that of a Christian perspective, which emerges as one theologically reflects. In considering self-esteem it appears that from a holistic perspective young people should at least be given the opportunity to accept or reject the concept of being made in the image of God and all the implications of a fully human Jesus. As Christian youth workers, are we acting in accordance with an understanding of salvation and shalom in denying young people the opportunity to engage with what for us is a truth? My role was to facilitate the student in having a reasoned answer to this question.

Sally used theological reflection as a methodology in a piece of research on urban youth workers. In listening to their experiences it soon became clear that measures of success such as the classic 'bums on seats' at a Sunday service were not helpful but that workers would benefit from reflection on ways in which their work was 'successful'. In thinking this through she chose to consider the idea of fruitfulness as a biblical way of interpreting the outcomes of work. In dialogue with workers this led on to an exploration of conditions that facilitate fruitfulness that could be adopted or contextualized by others entering this field. The experience of listening to these workers and using the parable of the sower as a starting point for discussion led to these conclusions:

- People need to be encouraged to explore and identify their calling and this calling needs to be tested and witnessed by others; often it is that sense of call that enables us to keep on going.
- Good preparation helps to clarify the call and equips the worker for their role. Apprenticeship-type approaches can be valuable (e.g. Jesus and his disciples; Eli and Samuel in 1 Samuel 3; Paul and Timothy in Acts 16.1–3) when encouraging more experienced workers to mentor those who are just starting out.
- People, like plants, flourish where the conditions are right and for any role in Christian ministry there are four facets that need to be considered: the workers themselves, the agency they work for, their management and support and the wider Christian community. All of these can hamper or enhance fruitfulness.
- A sustainable infrastructure helps workers in their task and frees them up to do what they are called to. This ranges from a shared

vision and strategy to an understanding that things such as networking are not optional extras.

- Balanced living is vital if a worker is to be there for the long haul. We have seen the added effectiveness of youth workers and other ministers who have been around for ten-plus years as the increased levels of trust, acceptance and relationships mean they are invited in to issues, people and places that others are not. Balanced living involves a rhythm of life that is sustainable and people often need time, support and permission to work out what that means.

These are some of the things that we would now encourage in a new youth project. There are quite a few more but this gives a flavour of what happens when we are theologically reflective and listen to the voice of experience and biblical and theological resources. (For the full version, see Nash, 2008.)

What is interesting to note about these two examples is that we often approach reflection differently. It reflects the way we take in information; Paul tends to be systematic and prefers to follow a step-by-step process and Sally tends to make connections and go off on tangents. Both are needed to be effective and it may be that we need to develop our skills more in one way of working than another.

Being theologically reflective enhances our practice of ministry and is a skill to equip others with too so they can make sense of their faith and experience in their daily lives and live in a way that feels authentic and integrated.

Frameworks for theological reflection

We are using the term framework to mean an approach to theological reflection. Tools such as those above can be used within the wider framework and, as Ballard and Pritchard point out, the only limit on what they are is probably our imagination (1996, p. 134). Subsequent chapters offer tools from a range of starting points and perspectives. Kinast (2000) categorizes frameworks or approaches to theological reflection into five main styles: ministerial, spiritual wisdom, feminist, inculturation and practical. We have summarized them in Table 2.2.

Such categories help us understand the broader context we are working in but will not always be helpful as we may have

Table 2.2 Kinast's styles of theological reflection (Kinast, 2000)

Style	Overview	Praxis
Ministerial	Theological reflection as 'the process of bringing to bear in the practical decisions of ministry the resources of the Christian faith' (p. 6). The minister draws on the faith tradition, personal and corporate experience and contemporary culture	Whitehead and Whitehead 'a pastoral response to the issue or concern that initiated the reflection in the first place' (p. 13)
Spiritual wisdom	Theological reflection in this tradition is rooted in everyday living for people of faith. It is possible for this approach to be used within a range of faith contexts	Killen and de Beer 'to carry people to deeper meaning and to a genuine relationship with their faith heritage' (p. 26)
Feminist	Theological reflection as a collaborative activity of both women and men that seeks 'to liberate the whole human community, especially the poor, in harmony with the earth from restrictive and destructive social structures and policies' (p. 27)	'emancipatory and transformative for both women and men, and the world that sustains them' (p. 38). A major focus is the liberation of women from oppression by men
Inculturation	Theological reflection originating from the cultural setting in which people are located. Originated mainly by missionaries working in non-Christian contexts. A stimulus for developing a local or contextual theology emerges as the primary reason for engaging in theological reflection	Schreiter 'a more effective and appropriate formation of Christian identity and response to social change' (p. 51)
Practical	Theological reflection from the field of practical theology which involves 'a critical theological reflection on current praxis rather than an application of theory to practice and it concentrates on the community of faith and its relationship to the larger society' (p. 52)	Ballard and Pritchard Transformational, 'it begins with a discrepancy between current praxis and belief, and it tries to overcome the discrepancy by proposing a more coherent theology and a more consistent praxis' (p. 63)

preconceived ideas or negative reactions to some of the words used. In seeking to identify and develop frameworks and tools for use in ministry we need to ensure that they are accessible and relevant to us and those we are using them with.

Conclusion

Theological reflection is about the God and kingdom we find in our everyday lives. Applied theology is about the God and kingdom principles we bring and seek to outwork in our everyday lives. We hope this chapter has explained the difference and extolled the virtues of adding theological reflection to our toolbox. Theological reflection should sometimes shock and surprise us because of what we learn about the God who is already there in our conversations, interventions and actions. Paul was out with our homegroup and saw a sign which said 'no effort, no entry', which struck him immediately as a challenge about his perspective on conversion and discipleship. Theological reflection gives us another tool in the box to get the job done, another well to drink from to be refreshed. It may not be the well in our homeland but we can travel to unfamiliar foreign territory and be replenished and not only survive but flourish.

Principles for theological reflection

- Expect to find God in everyday life.
- Be prepared to be shocked, surprised, inspired and challenged.
- Draw from as many faith wells as possible to make sense of your experience.
- Theological reflection is about the God we find in an experience engaging with the God we bring to it.
- Reflect prayerfully.

Benefits of theological reflection

- Encourages us to ask questions within a framework of faith.
- Helps and facilitates us to engage and draw upon our faith resources to process personal experiences, responses and pastoral episodes that trouble us.
- Encourages our faith to interact with our culture in mutual critique.

- Gives the possibility for the prophetic to emerge.
- Enables finding God and principles of the kingdom where we would least expect them.
- Deals with the big questions of life as well as everyday observations.
- Gives us a safe structure in which to engage with our deepest concerns.

? *What do you need to do now to become more of a theologically reflective practitioner?*

Part 2
CONTEXTS

3

Using metaphor in reflection

The mechanism by which spirituality becomes passionate is metaphor. An ineffable God requires metaphor not only to be imagined but to be approached, exhorted, evaded, confronted, struggled with, and loved. Through metaphor, the vividness, intensity, and meaningfulness of ordinary experience becomes the basis of a passionate spirituality. An effable God becomes vital through metaphor: The Supreme Being. The Prime Mover. The Creator. The Almighty. The Father. The King of Kings. Shepherd. Potter. Lawgiver. Judge. Mother. Lover. Breath.

(George Lakoff and Mark Johnson)

Perhaps the overgrown-ness of the garden is a metaphor for my life in this period of recovery [from major surgery]. There's all sorts of beautiful and fascinating things in there but a lot of clearing out may be necessary for them to emerge and flourish.

(Sally's journal, 6 December 2005)

Metaphors are all-pervasive, it is hard to read or watch something without being confronted by one. A metaphor is 'a figure of speech in which a name or descriptive word or phrase is transferred to an object or action different from, but analogous to, that to which it is literally applicable' or 'something regarded as representative or suggestive of something else, especially as a material emblem of an abstract quality, condition, notion, etc.; a symbol, a token' (*Oxford English Dictionary*, online, 2008). The root of the word is from the Greek *meta* meaning over or beyond and *pheirein* meaning to carry or transfer, leading to a definition of 'to carry a word over and beyond its original meaning by applying it to something else' (Grothe, 2008, p. 9). Green (1997, pp. 11–12) talks about seeing something through the screen of something else and watching to see what fits or doesn't. Grothe, in a similar vein, talks about metaphor as a 'magical mental changing room – where one thing, for a moment, becomes another and in that moment is seen in a whole new way' (2008, p. 10). He also offers a helpful overview of metaphor in relation to simile and analogy:

- An analogy says that A is to B as C is to D.
- A simile says that A is like B.
- A metaphor says that A is B or substitutes B for A (2008, p. 14).

Once we began to look for metaphors we were surprised how often they are used but have come to realize why. Metaphors are more than tools for reflection. According to Lakoff and Johnson (1980), they are part of our conceptual system, and are integral to the way that we think. They come to this view through linguistic analysis and, as an example, encourage us to reflect on what the difference would be between a culture that describes arguments using war metaphors and one that uses dance metaphors instead (1980, pp. 4–5) or the issues in a marriage where one thinks of it as a partnership and the other as a haven (1980, p. 243). Lakoff and Johnson's basic definition of a metaphor is 'understanding and experiencing one kind of thing in terms of another' (1980, p. 5). They offer a critique of how metaphor has previously been understood and emphasize the importance of seeing metaphors as conceptual rather than just a form of words (1980, pp. 244–6). Lakoff and Johnson summarize their theory of metaphor:

- Metaphors are fundamentally conceptual in nature; metaphorical language is secondary.
- Conceptual metaphors are grounded in everyday experience.
- Abstract thought is largely, though not entirely, metaphorical.
- Metaphorical thought is unavoidable, ubiquitous and mostly unconscious.
- Abstract concepts are not complete without metaphors. For example, love is not love without metaphors of magic, attraction, madness, union, nurture and so on.
- Our conceptual systems are not consistent overall, since the metaphors used to reason about concepts may be inconsistent.
- We live our lives on the basis of inferences we derive via metaphor (1980, pp. 272–3).

In showing what they mean they explore the idea of time as money, as a resource and as a valuable commodity, and list the ways we talk about time using metaphorical language:

- time as money: spend, invest, budget, use profitably, cost
- time as limited resources: use, use up, have enough of, run out of
- time as valuable commodity: have, give, lose, thank you for (1980, p. 9).

In ministry working out how we use time is a core skill, and watching how we talk and identifying the metaphors we use may help us see some of the patterns we adopt. If we find this idea that metaphor is an essential part of our thought processes valuable, then there are a wide range of other areas that merit reflecting on to help us understand at a deeper level how our thoughts and concepts impact the way that we live and work.

Process for reflecting with a metaphor

Metaphors are a particularly rich resource and tool for reflection to explore a range of issues as they give us new windows into areas we may be very familiar with:

- vocation
- ministry
- ministerial formation
- spiritual development
- leadership
- church
- relationships
- pastoral care
- teaching and preaching.

In the rest of this chapter there are many metaphors that can be used to gain insight on these areas of ministry. This is a process that can be used for reflecting with a metaphor or series of metaphors:

1 Pick an area of life and unpack the metaphors within that concept.
2 Choose one of these metaphors and explore all the connections the metaphor has for you. You may find it helpful to draw this.
3 Identify an area of your ministry to reflect on, for example, purpose of Church/ministry, leadership, nature of God, the lives of those you relate to, your view of the world.
4 Spend time sitting with your metaphor and your area of ministry and see what emerges.

5 Decide what your outcome(s) will be, for example, what you have
   learnt about yourself, how you want to minister, what you want
   to achieve.

Biblical metaphors

The Bible is full of metaphors. We have found it valuable to reflect
on which we are drawn to and which repel us. Such reflections help
us understand our philosophy of ministry and the elements that shape
us. One of Sally's favourites has always been the shepherd. It has
been slightly marred by the concept of 'heavy shepherding' with the
metaphor being misused as a tool for oppression rather than care.
For her, it is the seeking-out nature of the shepherd that first
attracted her but more recently it has been the challenge as a leader
to take heed of warnings in Ezekiel 34 about bad shepherds, which
has made her more aware of the potential for abuse. Green looks at
this metaphor in relation to Psalm 23 and Luke 15.3–7 and highlights
some of the issues raised when you begin to think about it. Reading
Green's reflections on the sheep and shepherd in Jesus and the blend
of responsibility and vulnerability (1997, p. 121) provided a new
insight for Sally to the Northumbria Community rule of availability
and vulnerability that she seeks to live by.

Understanding metaphor is an essential tool in working with biblical texts. McFague describes three types of metaphor. The first is
poetic metaphor, which is about creating new meaning. The second,
radical metaphor is about metaphor being constitutive of language.
This echoes Lakoff and Johnson's claim that metaphor is integral to
the way we think and speak. The third is metaphor as human movement, which is about metaphor being the method of knowledge
development (1975, p. 36). McFague has developed guidelines in relation to using metaphor:

- The various forms of metaphorical language operative in biblical
  literature and in the Christian literary tradition ought to be
  looked at carefully as resources for theological reflection.
- These forms are not secondary embellishments to the mainline systematic and doctrinal tradition, but are, in fact, its nourishment.
- Recognizing the importance of such forms as parable, story,
  poem, and confession does not imply substituting these forms for

systematic theology, but it does imply a continuum from these forms to systematic theology (1975, p. 53).

Such guidelines help provide parameters for using metaphor in our reflection and study. We have found that the easiest way of helping students to understand and apply doctrine in their youth work practice is to start with a metaphor, for example, to ask: What is redemption in your context?

When we think about the Bible, themes emerge that we clearly use in a metaphorical way. For example, from the Old Testament we talk about Eden, the ark, the flood, exodus, desert, wilderness, mountain top, exile, Jezebel, Job's comforter. The New Testament has many uses of metaphorical language, for example, the 'I ams' of Jesus: bread (John 6.35), light (John 8.12), gate (John 10.7), good shepherd (John 10.11), resurrection and the life (John 11.25), the way, the truth, the life (John 14.6), the true vine (John 15.1). The parables offer a range of metaphors, such as weeds (Matthew 13.24–30), sheep and goats (Matthew 25.31–46), growing seed (Mark 4.26–29), house on the rock (Luke 6.47–49), debtors (Luke 7.41–43), sower (Luke 8.5–8), good Samaritan (Luke 10.30–37), faithful steward (Luke 12.42–48), mustard seed (Luke 13.18–19), leaven (Luke 13.20–21), banquet (Luke 14.16–24), lost sheep (Luke 15.4–6), talents (Luke 19.12–27). Paul uses language such as a race (1 Corinthians 9.24), prize (Philippians 3.14), armour (Romans 13.12; Ephesians 6.11), thorn in the flesh (2 Corinthians 12.7), body of Christ (1 Corinthians 12.12f.).

Danny did an interesting exercise with young people and got them to reframe the 'I ams' of Jesus into concepts that resonate

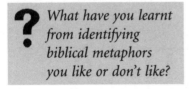
What have you learnt from identifying biblical metaphors you like or don't like?

with them. They came up with ideas such as police officer and lollipop, which give fascinating insights into how they see Jesus and may alert a youth worker to ways in which we may have mis-

represented him in our teaching or a bias that comes through in our worship songs that we can then address.

Metaphors of ministry and priesthood

We explore metaphors of ministry and priesthood in teaching ministerial formation. We give the students a copy of Table 3.1, which

Table 3.1 Metaphors of ministry and priesthood

Bennett (biblical)	O'Leary	Dwinell	Monbourquette archetypes	Pritchard	Paul and Sally
Prophet	Farmer of hearts	Hero	Sage	Presiding genius	Nestbuilder
Priest	Prophet of beauty	Fool	Leader	Spiritual explorer	Roller coaster
King	Healer of fear	Mother and child	Mentor	Artful storyteller	Fit
Servant	Midwife of mystery	Wound	Protective parent	Multilingual interpreter	Robbed, mugged
Shepherd	Soul-friend of community	Silence	Manager	Inquisitive learner	Hijacked
Worker	Weaver of wholeness	Sinner	Healer	Pain-bearer	Balancing act
Apostle	Voice of the silent	Courageous coward	Artist	Wounded companion	Public property
Messenger	Sacrament of compassion	Servant of ceremony	Seeker	Weather-beaten	Goldfish bowl
Ambassador		Death's friend	Disciple	Iconic presence	Pressure cooker
Soldier		Nexus	Magician/sorceress	Friendly irritant	Shelter
Witness			Psychologist	Creative leader	Signposts

Bennett (biblical)	O'Leary	Dwinell	Monbourquette archetypes	Pritchard	Paul and Sally
Athlete			Ambassador	Attractive witness	Refiner
Teacher			Wilderness person	Faith coach	Growbag
Prophet			Fool	Mature risk taker	Boundaries
Chosen			Hero/heroine	Flower arranger	Replenisher
Fisherman			Warrior	Life-fulfiller	Marathon
Salt			Lover		Triage
Soil			Contemplative		Scapegoat
Friend			Prophet		Fallow time
Branch			Celebrant		Ebb and flow
Disciple			Eternal child		Accumulate
Child					Security
Manager					GP
Light					Baby and bathwater
Seed					Friendly fire

Sources: Bennett (1993); O'Leary (1997); Monbourquette (2003); Pritchard (2007)

summarizes various authors' metaphors and then ask each person in the group (they have been together for over two years) to choose five they identify with. We collect them up and then read them out and people have to guess whose they are. From what you have read so far, you might like to try to guess which of us is: wounded companion, healer of fear, faith coach, death's friend and friendly irritant? As well as encouraging people to reflect on those they resonate with we suggest they identify and articulate some of their own.

We both resonate with the idea of the wounded healer (Nouwen, 1994) who is working towards becoming more whole. There was a joke running between Paul and a group of students where Sally was referred to as the oracle, a metaphor she preferred to reject although she has always liked the cartoon character Snoopy who sometimes functions in that way. Sometimes metaphors can uncover elements of us that we are not aware of or aspects of us that we try to overlook. For Sally, competence is important. The oracle, as in someone who could answer lots of questions, touches on this and helps her understand how others may perceive her and may help her come to terms with the fact that she is now moving towards old wise woman status. On another occasion Sally reflected on aspects of her ministry as a snowdrop; she blossoms in situations where others perhaps don't and in seasons when there are fewer flowers around. This helped her accept some of her uniqueness. Paul sometimes experiences hospital chaplaincy as International Rescue (*Thunderbirds*) and has become more conscious of not giving false hope. He tries to be conscious of being a Godbearer in that context, which impacts the way he behaves as for many people he is the only representative of Christ that people may have encountered personally.

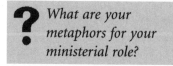
What are your metaphors for your ministerial role?

Along with metaphors for ministerial roles, we also work with metaphors that relate more to the ministry context and content. The 'wells' metaphor mentioned in the previous chapter resonates with Paul. He likes the idea of depth, of drawing water that is already there, that refreshes. We are also aware of sacred wells and the idea that wells are places where God is present and sometimes supernatural things occur. This was reinforced when Sally bathed her feet in St Non's well and experienced over subsequent weeks significant healing of a foot problem.

It can be easy to dismiss or ignore history and tradition and for us the concept of wells particularly brings that to mind as we reflect on what ministry means for us.

Josh works with Nick, a young person whose favourite pastime is watching wrestling on television; wrestling is the highlight of his viewing week. Josh likes the story of Jacob wrestling with God and not letting go until he had got what he wanted and sees it as a good reminder that doing ministry can sometimes be a long and hard task. It shows how struggle and engagement are an integral part of ministry and helps with being patient and persevering for the long haul. Unfortunately what Nick enjoys about wrestling and how Josh might want to draw upon it in thinking about ministry are two very different things! This contradiction also reminds us that images and symbols change over time and when using them with a group we may need to establish understandings of the concept first.

The metaphor of the elephant in the room is relevant in so many ways in ministry. It features in a well-known poem about how it feels to a bereaved family when their loss is not talked about ('The Elephant in the Room' by Terry Kettering). Paul has been struck by the powerful feelings this poem evokes and he uses it in other contexts. He has used it to explore resource allocation and the lack of resources in medical ethics. He parallels resource allocation as the elephant in the room that no one wants to talk about.

> **?** *What is the elephant in your church, personal life, family, fear, community? Does someone need to acknowledge it? Should it be you?*

Life-shaping metaphors

If we agree with the premise that metaphors are part of our conceptual system then it is likely that we will encounter or have encountered metaphors that have shaped our lives. Grothe (2008, ch. 1) offers some of his and talks about how he has collected such sayings over the years. These are some which seem pertinent to ministry:

> I wanted to live deep and suck all the marrow out of life and Dwell as near as possible to the channel in which your life flows.
> (Henry David Thoreau, a nineteenth-century American author)

The Promised Land always lies on the other side of a Wilderness.
(Havelock Ellis, a twentieth-century English psychologist)

Sometimes our light goes out but is blown again into flame by an encounter with another human being. Each of us owes deepest thanks to those who have rekindled this inner light.
(Albert Schweitzer, born in Alsace and best known as a medical missionary in Africa)

Don't judge each day by the harvest you reap, but by the seeds you plant.
(Robert Louis Stevenson, a nineteenth-century Scottish author)

> **?** *Do you have life-shaping metaphors? Does your church or agency? How has this influenced your ministerial formation?*

In our contemporary culture it may be songs, films or other items from popular culture that have provided us with the metaphors that have helped shape our identity and ministry. Sometimes we draw a timeline of significant events in our life; perhaps we should do a similar exercise but try and recall what were the significant stories, sayings, songs and so on that have influenced us. Some of ours are win-win, salt and light, field of dreams, tides and seasons, gate of the year, entertaining angels.

Transferred metaphors

Our experience in one area may give us a rich source of metaphor. Because Paul works in a hospital, metaphors of health, healing, illness and death often come to mind. For example, he has been reflecting on issues and problems as illness or tumours. Thus taking the body metaphor (1 Corinthians 12), what illness does the body have, or where is the tumour? Is there a limb that is broken? What stage is the illness in – recovery or is it terminal? Steve is a chef and got used to preparing oysters and the idea that some of the people he encounters are the grit that creates the pearl (in terms of refining his reactions and attitudes) works for him. Suki enjoys walking, which leads to questions such as what or where are our mountains, valleys, light, signposts, map, café, stiles, companions and so on. Other sources of metaphor include:

- *weather/nature* seasons, tsunami, storm, shelter, frost, drought, eclipse, darkness, volcano, black hole, flood, iceberg, snow . . .
- *relationships/roles* parent, police, child, divorce, apprentice, backing vocalist, best friend, enemy, knight, miner . . .
- *travel* motorway, dead end, baggage, flying, security, hijacked, signpost, one-way street, cul-de-sac, footpath, sleigh, transporter, breakdown . . .
- *housing* foundations, windows, open door, mansion, tent, freehold, tower, attic, cellar, balcony, staircase, kitchen, bathroom . . .
- *food* feeding, raw, pressure cooker, hunger, nourishment, poisoning, snack, staples, carnivore, vegetarian, vitamins, chocolate, comfort food . . .
- *medical* transplant, medication, hospital, stillbirth, GP, triage, infected, drowning, burn, A&E, scar tissue, conception, oxygen, resuscitate, plaster, pill . . .
- *business* brand, counterfeit, accumulate, public property, investment, patent, loss, profit, bankrupt, tax . . .
- *leadership* manager, coach, CEO, servant, trailblazer, pacesetter, shepherd, monarch, dictator, president, captain, figurehead . . .
- *sport* competition, referee, rules, game, marathon, sprint, spectators, injury, win, lose, draw, playing field, cheating, sportsmanship, professional foul, time out, extra time, substitute, champion, penalties . . .
- *the sea* lifeboat, harbours, anchor, capsize, rescue, repairing nets, ebb and flow, lighthouse, seaweed, shore, driftwood, wave, drown, rock pool, shark, whale, starfish . . .
- *farming/gardening* pruning, growbag, fertilizer, fallow time, watering, sow, fruit, reap, dig, milk, propagate, harvest, crop failure . . .
- *war* enemy, friendly fire, prisoner, killed, grave, fight, assassinate, bomb, protect, liberate, defend . . .
- *circus* tightrope, safety net, clown, lion tamer, acrobat, ringmaster . . .
- *social* abuse, obese, invisible, poverty, mugged, stolen, abandoned, immigration, pollution, gated complex, crime, neighbour . . .
- *sayings* throwing the baby out with the bath water, give them enough rope to hang themselves, get in step, fault line, bite off more than you can chew, sinking sand, spectator sport . . .
- *theological* e.g. salvation: saved, born again, purchased, found, rescued, redeemed . . .

- *miscellaneous* roller coaster, scapegoat, balancing act, goldfish bowl, mini me, conduit, catalyst, evolution, gagged, treasure, dream, magnet, invisible, source of energy, mask, open door, giants, joke, renewable energy/solar power, declutter, control, refuge, shackles, pawn, desert, orbit, parachute, empty vessel . . .

> **?** *Do your background or interests lead you to a particular family of metaphors? What are the implications of this?*

Poetic metaphors

Poems and songs are a fruitful source of metaphor. We were introduced to the Christian band Note for a Child by a friend and their song 'Impossibly beautiful' uses metaphor powerfully to describe a relationship:

> I am the question and you are the answer
> I am the lyric with words who like dancers
> Need you, the melody, to give life to my song.
> I am a boat in the sea all alone
> You are the North Star guiding me home
> I'm the explorer and you are the treasure I seek . . .
> I am a Japanese house made of paper
> You, like a hurricane, lay me to waste
> Here in my brokenness
> Everything changes but you.
>
> (Goodman, 2000)

When it is hard to find language to talk about what you feel then metaphor can bring shades of meaning that give life. Sally still remembers a poem she learnt about 30 years ago where the author talks about sleep and the anticipation of the next day's challenges: ''til falling forward, trackless, unknowing down a slope, you're there sitting in it, you and hope' ('Lord's Test', Snow, 1973). Reciting the poem in her head helps reassure her that others may be feeling the same about a forthcoming event.

For further reflection

Use the following questions or statements to trigger your own reflection:

- Boom–bust: church or personal walk with God.
- Guidance: map or satellite navigation system?
- Do you want to be a pontoon, pier, bridge or stepping stone?
- What game or toy are you?
- Where and how do you and others sacrifice?

Conclusion

This chapter has sought to introduce the concept of metaphor and some thinking around its use. There are examples of metaphor in most of the other chapters, which perhaps reinforces the point about how significant they are for our thinking. They provide another lens for our reflection and often bring fresh and surprising insights. Listen out in conversations and to different media for metaphors as they give clues on how people think and can also act as triggers to us for our reflection. Giving time to exploring the metaphors that have affected and do influence our ministry or our community brings insights that help us be more effective and self-aware. We love metaphors and hope they will bring fresh food to your diet, a new dish to your menu. Okay, we'll stop now.

? *How would you describe your ministry in metaphorical terms?*

4

Spiritual practices for reflection

I looked out of the window. All I could see was a fence and a few cars and mist, yet I knew that beyond the mist was a tidal estuary and if the mist ever lifted the view was stunning. This is not dissimilar to how I have felt at different points on my journey. It felt like I was in mist, there was nothing really wrong yet there was a sense of frustration, a feeling that there might be more out there. I wanted to move beyond where I was.

(Reflection while writing some of this chapter)

I have observed that when I am most discouraged and am finding my pastoral work more dreary than joyful, a gradual and dangerous shift has taken place in my thinking about myself. I forget that I am a Christian who has found in Christ a resting-place. The truth that I am a person who, despite my sinfulness, has been accepted and acquitted through faith in the Lord Jesus Christ is neglected. I seem to become strangely unaware that I have been made by sheer grace on God's part, a child of God; that he has given me the gift of his Spirit and that I have experienced the reality of both his presence and power in my life and work.

(Brain, 2004, p. 245)

Most of us will have got to either or both of these places in our ministry and although other ways of reflecting described in this book may help, spiritual practices can be particularly helpful in nurturing our spirit and soul. However, there is a part of us that resists using the term spiritual practice in this book as it can imply a false dichotomy that suggests that the reflective practices in this chapter are somehow 'better' than those in other chapters because they are more overtly connected with God. Some practices we make spiritual by the focus and content. For example, we both make resolutions or promises. Sally's tend to be the classic new year ones that involve losing weight and other such things (as well as some spiritual ones); whereas Paul does his at other times, Advent (the beginning of the church year) or Lent, for example, and his tend to be ministry-focused, for example, 'some things matter more and I need to give time to those things'. In whatever ways we do connect with God we need to give time to deepening that relationship. 'The more you are called to speak for God's love, the more you will need to deepen the knowledge of love in your own heart. The farther the outward journey takes you, the deeper the inner journey must be' (Nouwen, 1996, pp. 93–4). Reflective spiritual practices help us go deeper.

Reflecting with the Bible

There are many different ways of reading the Bible and here we are highlighting some that facilitate reflection.

Imaginative contemplation

This approach to reading the Bible is an aspect of Ignatian spirituality. Ignatius of Loyola was the founder of the Jesuits. He was born in 1491 in the Basque region of Spain and published his *Spiritual Exercises* in 1548. Ignatius uses the terms consolation and desolation to describe the feelings these exercises evoke. Consolation may include feelings such as joy, hope, happiness, contentment, affirmation and life while desolation may include despair, disquiet, frustration, sorrow, turmoil, anxiety, fear, death. Feelings in this context are neither right nor wrong but indications of what is happening in our inner lives and they thus merit spending time with. Don't always assume that desolation is negative as it can serve a fruitful purpose in our reflection, for example, it can be a prompt to move on or make a change. However, in our training as Ignatian prayer guides we were exhorted not to change a decision made in a period of consolation when in a time of desolation.

Step 1

Choose a passage from the Bible; normally this would be a story from the Gospels which involves an encounter with Jesus (some suggestions are listed below under 'suggested passages for reflection' on pp. 76–8). Decide how long you want to spend in prayer and try to stick to that time (20 minutes is a good starting place). Read the passage through a few times before you start.

Step 2

Ask God for what you want to happen. This may be:

- to recognize and acknowledge what Jesus is doing in your life at the moment
- to express your love and gratitude to Jesus
- to hear what Jesus is saying to you now
- to consider where you are in your spiritual journey.

Step 3

Use your imagination to picture the scene.

Steps 4 to 7 are not necessarily chronological; pursue them as seems right for you.

Step 4

Use your five senses of sight, hearing, taste, smell and touch to explore the scene.

- Where is the scene located?
- What can you see?
- Picture the people in the scene:
  - Who are they? What are their lives like?
  - What do they feel?
  - What factors (physical, social, spiritual, emotional, economic, etc.) are affecting their lives?
  - What hopes and emotions do they bring with them to this scene?

Step 5

Listen to their conversation.

- What dialogue comes before and after the Scripture as well as during the story?
- What is their tone of voice? What emotions are being expressed?
- Who is involved? Who is just watching?

Step 6

See how the people act.

- What do you think their motives are?
- Do their actions have any implications for you today?
- How does what is happening fit into the bigger picture?

Step 7

Imagine yourself as one of the characters in the reading. Enter into dialogue with the people in your scene, especially Jesus. If this is difficult, imagine what someone else might say to them.

Step 8

Leave the scene when it seems right to do so. Consider what has happened during this time. What images, words or phrases struck you? How did you feel before, during and after the time of prayer? What, if anything, distracted you? Take what you think God may be saying to you through it, reflect on it and test it. Try and summarize in your journal what you think has happened or been revealed to you and talk it through with someone if this is appropriate.

A passage Sally revisits regularly is Jesus at the home of Martha and Mary (Luke 10.38–42). One of the things that has struck her more than once is the tension between being a Martha and a Mary. Thus, spending time with the passage as this book was nearly written led to Sally noticing that she was looking with envy at Mary who was sitting at the feet of Jesus but also that she reacted negatively to Martha going and complaining, because Martha had chosen what to do in this situation. This resonated with Sally who knew she had chosen to write a book and would therefore be busier than usual and only she could take responsibility for this decision; thus, she should not complain. However, she realized that she was like Martha at times and complained to those close to her when no one but she herself could do anything about the situation – facing the reality of some of our less helpful characteristics sometimes needs honest reflection. The time finished with a dialogue between Sally and Jesus talking about taking time in Advent and exploring a new way of spending time with Jesus that would provide that sense of peace and space. On other occasions the Holy Spirit has led her into reflections that have focused around hospitality, ways of listening to Jesus and what service and ministry mean.

Lectio divina

When we read the Bible we are looking for God to speak to us in the here and now. *Lectio divina* is a technique which involves reading, meditating and praying. This is also known as meditative or spiritual reading. It is a slow reading that savours the words of the passage; some describe it as listening with heart.

Step 1   *Silencio* Begin with a period of silence to still yourself before beginning the exercise.

Step 2   *Lectio* Choose a passage that connects with what you want to explore. We use the list on pages 76–8 as a guide and ask the Holy Spirit to lead us to the right passage for us at that time. Read it through several times then . . .

Step 3   *Meditatio* Begin to read slowly. As soon as a word or phrase or thought leaps out at you or resonates with you then stay with it, let it permeate your subconscious.

Step 4   *Oratio* Pray, respond, dialogue, reflect to let the word or image do its work in you. Continue to be open to what God is saying.

Step 5   *Contemplatio* Spend a while resting in God's presence.

At the end of the time record what you think God has been saying, making a special note of any feelings or thoughts you think need further reflection or talk over the experience with someone else. Depending on their church tradition we may also encourage people to read until the Holy Spirit enlivens a word or verse to them with the expectation that God wants to speak to them through the exercise. This needs to be done in an attitude of openness and a willingness to hear what we may not want to. As always, use discernment criteria to check out what emerges. As we have broadened our experience of other Christian traditions we have often found that processes are similar but the words used to describe them are different.

Reading into the story

Writing or acting out a Bible passage from a variety of perspectives may help us get into the story and draw out fresh insights. We can write it in the first person, as a poem or narrative story or add some of the details that the original account leaves out. We can improvise it dramatically, draw it or use one of the other approaches described in this chapter. Here are a couple of examples. The first is a poem called 'Peter's fire' and the second is some reflections from Henri

Nouwen on the same story from John 21. These are also the sort of reflections that may emerge from imaginative contemplation.

> And yet . . .
> On the far horizon of his pain,
> barely visible across the valley of death,
> a distant fire was already being kindled,
> not by men but by God himself.
> In the bright light of a Galilee morning
> breakfast was sizzling,
> prepared by One who was still dying to serve them,
> the towel round his waist
> exchanged for a cooking apron.
> Food for hungry hearts, cooked not on a fire
> made of wood and tangled thorns,
> but a fire of burning coals,
> heaping goodness upon their heads.
> And at last Peter's heart began to thaw,
> his failure transformed in the furnace
> of God's forgiveness,
> loved into life.
> Instead of protesting at this foot-washing Messiah,
> who insisted on loving and cooking
> and serving them breakfast,
> he allowed his spirit to be re-kindled with love,
> fanned into resurrection flame.
> So when the apron was offered,
> he accepted it with joy,
> trusting that the recipes for sheep-feeding would be
> given in due course,
> when he needed them.
> (Calvert, in Watterson, 2006, pp. 42–3)

The question from Jesus to Peter is not: How many people take you seriously? How much are you going to accomplish? Can you show some results? But: Are you in love with Jesus? Perhaps another way of putting the question would be: Do you know the incarnate God? In our world there is an enormous need for men and women who know the heart of God, a heart that forgives, that cares, that reaches out and wants to heal . . . Knowing God's heart means consistently, radically, and very concretely to announce and reveal that God is love and only love, and that every time fear, isolation or despair begin to invade the human soul this is not something that comes from God. This sounds very simple and maybe even trite, but very few people know that they are loved without any conditions or limits.

(Nouwen, 2001, pp. 125–6)

Suggested passages for reflection

For the imaginative contemplation you need to choose a passage about people, we frequently use those under the heading 'Encounters with Jesus'. Any of these passages can be used for *lectio divina*.

Questions and invitations

Matthew 11.28–30 Come to me . . .
Matthew 16.13–16 Who do you say that I am?
Mark 10.46–52 What do you want me to do for you?
John 1.35–39 What do you want?
John 5.1–9 Do you want to get well?
John 21.15–19 Do you love me?

Challenges

Deuteronomy 30.15–20 Choose life
Proverbs 3 Trust in the Lord
Micah 6.8 Act justly . . .
Matthew 16.24–28 If anyone would follow
Matthew 28.16–20 The Great Commission – Go . . .
Luke 10.38–42 Mary and Martha – choosing the better thing
Luke 22.14–20 Do this in remembrance of me
Luke 24.44–53 Commissioning
John 2.1–12 Do whatever he tells you
John 13.1–17 Do as I have done for you
John 21.15–19 Take care of my sheep
Romans 12.1–2 Transformed by the renewing of your mind
Colossians 3.1–11 Set your hearts on things above
1 Thessalonians 5.12–24 Live in peace with each other

Encounters with Jesus

Matthew 8.5–13 The centurion
Matthew 8.23–27 The calming of the storm
Matthew 16.13–18, 23 Jesus and Peter
Matthew 19.13–15 Children and Jesus

Mark 10.17–27 The rich young man
Mark 10.46–52 Blind Bartimaeus
Luke 2.41–50 Jesus in the Temple
Luke 4.23–30 Jesus experiencing rejection
Luke 8.43–48 Woman who was bleeding
Luke 19.1–10 Zacchaeus
Luke 24.13–35 The Emmaus Road
John 5.1–9 Healing at the pool
John 11.38–44 Lazarus raised from the dead
John 20.11–18 Mary in the garden
John 20.19–23 Disciples
Philippians 2.5–11 Became as a slave

Seeking God

Deuteronomy 30.11–14 The word is very near you
1 Kings 19.9–13 The still small voice
Psalm 40 I waited patiently

Guidance and calling

Genesis 12.1–3 Call of Abraham
Exodus 3 Moses and the burning bush
Ruth 1 Introducing Ruth
1 Samuel 3.1–14 Call of Samuel
1 Samuel 16 Call of David
Esther 2 Introducing Esther
Ecclesiastes 3.1–8 A time for everything
Isaiah 6 Call of Isaiah
Isaiah 52.7–12 How beautiful on the mountains
Jeremiah 1 Call of Jeremiah
Ezekiel 2—3 Call of Ezekiel
Daniel 1 Daniel's consecration
Matthew 4.18–22, Mark 1.14–20, Luke 5.1–11 Call of the disciples
Matthew 13.1–23 Parable of the sower
Matthew 25.14–30 Parable of the talents
Luke 1.26–56 Call of Mary
Luke 14.25–35 Cost of being a disciple
Acts 9.1–19 Conversion of Paul

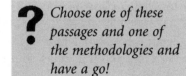

Choose one of these passages and one of the methodologies and have a go!

1 Corinthians 1.26–31 Not many wise . . .
2 Thessalonians 2.13–17 Called through the gospel
1 Timothy 6.11–21 Call of Timothy
1 Peter 2.4–12 Living stones

Sources from our Christian heritage

If we had remained the same size since our teenage years we would rarely have had to buy new clothes as fashions tend to come round again and again. It sometimes seems like that in our Christian experience. It is often said that to understand the present we need to be aware of what has happened in the past. Exploring our Christian heritage can be a fruitful source for reflection. Hebrews 12.1 talks about the great cloud of witnesses that surround us as we seek to run the race set before us. We can learn from them too and stories of saints and others can be sources of comfort, strength and inspiration.

The examen

Another Ignatian practice we find helpful is the examen. It can be used in many ways to develop and sustain our ministry. The examen is more fully called the examination of conscience or consciousness or the awareness examen. In using the examen we can apply the insights to our relationship with God, to our relationship to ourself or self-awareness, and to our relationship with others. The premise of the examen is that we trust God and the Holy Spirit to bring to mind those things which we need to focus on, work through, become aware of and so on. The examen can be used in a variety of different ways and contexts such as:

- putting to bed a day – dealing with feelings or experiences that we have not had an opportunity to process or which we were not aware of until later or which needed resolution;
- dealing with an incident or experience that we were concerned about at the time;
- providing a structure for reflective practice;
- in providing a holistic exploration of issues that incorporates both consolation and desolation;
- as a tool and framework for dialogue in supervision or spiritual direction;

- allowing the Holy Spirit to bring new insights and fresh perceptions.

A basic examen process

1 It is probably best to keep some record of thoughts and obser-vations. What will begin to emerge will be patterns, a flow, which will hopefully point out a consistency to what brings life or death. Insight comes the more often we do the exercise, as we draw on different activities, experiences, days, weeks, moods, etc.
2 Take time, in a quiet place with no distractions, to sit and reflect on the past day/week/month or other period. Allow at least 20 minutes for the process; it may take longer depending on how far in time you go back.
3 Ask the questions below or other questions that seem relevant. Be honest, don't judge what comes to mind. Don't sift out what seems good or bad. Accept the thoughts, jot them down and sit with them and see if they reflect your truest feelings.
   - Where/when did you find consolation/joy/life or feel alive/feel recharged/contentment?
   - Where/when did you find desolation/death/draining/despair/frustration/sorrow?
4 Review the answers to questions such as these:
   - Where are the most powerful memories/feelings?
   - What were you doing?
   - Who were you with?
   - Was there a single event that comes to mind when you ask the questions?
   - What contexts are you exploring – relationship with God, self or others?
   - Is there any action you need to take out of this reflection?
   Thank God for the good things and ask for God's help in the difficult situation and say sorry where necessary.
5 As you do this over a few days, weeks, months, ask yourself:
   - Do any patterns emerge?
   - Are there any constants?
   - Is any change being called for?
   - What might this say about how I might best serve God?

We have found several benefits of using the examen. One is that it gives a structure around discernment and reflection. It can encourage the development of a discipline in doing this regularly rather than just in crisis or it can provide a starting point for people who do not know where to begin in seeking to make a decision. A benefit is that we have to engage with both consolation and desolation. For those who have a tendency to focus on only one it helps bring a more rounded reflection.

Susan was unhappy at work. An illness had meant that she had been redeployed into a different department and she came to talk about this. She had also had no real choice in the new job she was given and it did not connect with any of her interests, motivations or preferred way of working. The illness had made pursuing her original career impossible and in diagnosing the situation Paul felt that encouraging her to identify other ways of working out her original motivations might be helpful. They met four or five times to explore the process. One discovery was that she found consolation in helping people, being practical, having a variety of work, being able to use her own initiative, and interacting with others. Desolation involved doing things upfront, getting stuck into a routine with little variety, being treated with less respect than in her previous role, feeling frustrated that her contribution now didn't bring the same recognition and satisfaction and missing the contact she had previously had with service users. During this process a post became available which matched what had emerged in the examen process. She applied and got the job!

> **?** *Is there an issue that you need to explore using the examen?*

Exploring our vocation

Knowing and understanding our vocation is fundamental to our lives. Both of us have an idea of some of our core gifts and calling but the places and ways they are worked out have changed over time. In ministry it can be fruitful periodically to reflect on our vocation and these are some of the ways we do this beginning with the premise from Ephesians 2.10, 'For we are what he has made us, created in Christ Jesus for good works, which God prepared beforehand to be our way of life.' Along with encouraging the use of the examen, these are some of the questions that we ask:

- What has God called you to do? What is your mission in life?
- How would you answer if you were to finish the sentence from Luke 4.18, 'The Spirit of the Lord is on me, because he has anointed me to . . .'
- What do you want to achieve through your ministry?
- Which dreams and visions are not yet fulfilled?
- What are the principles you want to live and minister by?
- What does it mean for you or the people you minister alongside to have 'life in all its fullness' (John 10.10, *GNB*)?
- Which biblical concepts or theological themes have shaped your understanding of ministry? How has this changed over the years?
- Which metaphors best describe your ministry?
- What has happened to hold you back in ministry? What are you doing about these areas?
- Have you experienced any paradigm shifts that have impacted your vocation or ministry?
- At the end of your life what will be important?

Vocation is one of those concepts which can be fraught with difficulty. We have met people in the past who have a 'plan a' theology and if something goes wrong and diverts them from this then it is on to 'plan b' and so on. This can be oppressive. Jones offers an interesting exercise which moves us away from this idea:

> In a dream you are somewhat startled to hear God say, 'Thank you for being so considerate of my will. But you know, more than anything else, my will is for you to do what you really desire doing.' Awakening with God's words fresh in your mind, you go to a table and begin writing freely on a sheet of paper, 'What I'd really enjoy doing is . . .' (2007, p. 29)

Probably the most beneficial book for us on this topic is *Sleeping with Bread* (Linn *et al.*, 1995). The concept of doing what brings us life has been liberating although there is still the evangelical bit of us that adds 'and thy will be done, Lord'. Ultimately we both believe that God has created us, called us, given us gifts and that he will guide us and lead us as to where these gifts will be worked out but that often the choice is ours. As our hearts grow more and more attentive to the moving of the Holy Spirit then it will become harder to discern between our choice and God's and, hopefully, much of the time they will be the same thing.

Silence and solitude

A friend came round to see us. His teenage daughter had recently left home and he was saying, 'Remember when I said I hate being on my own? Well, I love it now, I really love it.' Silence can take a bit of getting used to and to us, coming from a generation where the radio or television was a constant in the background, silence felt a little strange at first. The example of Jesus in taking time to withdraw and spend time alone is one for us to follow; 'silence is the seedbed of the creative life, a preparation for utterance or action' (Leckey, 1999, p. 44). We can create silent places in our own homes or enjoy the deep silence to be found in churches and other sacred places. One of the delights of a rural holiday is that many churches are still open all day and we can go in and drink in the peace and tranquillity. In the youth work world, contemplative spirituality is having a resurgence and young people are being introduced to the value of spending time in silence. One of the dilemmas of time in silence and solitude is that it can feel like we are wasting time or being selfish. However, time spent in silence and solitude can help us be more productive in the rest of our lives. Goff uses the term 'creative balancing' to describe the rhythm that Jesus demonstrates and suggests that our soul needs a balance of 'retreat and involvement, silence and speech, resting and risking' (1993, p. 74) to flourish.

Centring prayer is a way into exploring silence. It is based on the idea of Psalm 46.10: 'Be still, and know that I am God!' We take a word or short phrase such as Jesus, God, Father, Mother, peace, faith, trust, be still, Jesus is Lord, come, Holy Spirit, and repeat it to ourselves; in doing this we are inviting God to be present and active with us. Some suggest different postures as appropriate and helpful although we tend to go with what feels comfortable and often that is our recliner chair! Often thoughts, images and so on will emerge; this is usual and we return to our word or phrase. At the end of the time of centring prayer it can be helpful to sit in silence for a couple of minutes. For further information see <http://www.centeringprayer.com/methodcp.htm>.

Sabbath

'Remember the sabbath day, and keep it holy. For six days you shall labour and do all your work' (Exodus 20.8–9). Once Paul started in a parish, Sabbath became an important concept to us. Up until that point we had most weekends and could balance everything well. With a one-day-off, busy curate's lifestyle we revisited the idea of the Sabbath. For us it couldn't be Sunday as that was a workday so we had to find an alternative. Whitcomb talks about Sabbath being a day of being rather than doing:

> When I was young, I believed that Sabbath was an unproductive waste of time: good works and hard work seemed to be more effective and more laudable. Now in my middle age, when the quickly evident fruits of non-sabbath appear in the form of witheredness, weariness, and despair, I am newly in love with the necessity of Sabbath.
>
> (2002, p. 14)

What is Sabbath time depends on who we are. For us it starts with breakfast together, usually out somewhere and this is where we get to talk about things we may not have had time to do in the week. Then it tends to be a relaxed lunch with friends, a walk and home for pizza and a film. Housework and other work tends to be ignored for that day! That's what recharges us; it is our version of a day of rest. It's enjoying the bits of life that can get squeezed out of most of the other days of the week and enjoying God's creation and provision. Goff suggests that Sabbath time is about us being prayerful, playful and passionate (1993, p. 79), and we want some of that! Looking at the bigger picture Calhoun reminds us that Sabbath is about us being:

? *How do you do Sabbath? Do you need to make changes to make it more nourishing?*

> citizens of another kingdom – a kingdom not ruled by the clock and the tyranny of the urgent. God's Sabbath reality calls us to trust that the Creator can manage all that concerns us in this world as we settle into his rest. (2005, p. 42)

Places of pilgrimage

Places of pilgrimage can provide us with extra special opportunities for reflection as we can feel particularly close to God there. We try each year to visit at least one place of pilgrimage, even if it is just for a day, although we try to have a retreat somewhere significant too. The phrase 'thin place' is often used to describe such places; it is as if we are closer to heaven and can hear and experience God more readily.

One of our favourite places of pilgrimage is Holy Island, particularly the pilgrim's walk across the sand at low tide, following the marker posts, seeing the shelters. We have done the walk several times and Paul has stayed in a shelter over a high tide. This is part of his reflection on the journey:

> One of the things I realized was that we need both marker posts and shelters on our journey. They serve different purposes, the marker posts guide us and lead us and show us where we are going. The shelter provides a place to be when you cannot see where you are going or the journey is too dangerous or you are just too tired to carry on. As individuals and as churches we need to be both marker posts and shelters, to help people on their journey, to find the way that's right for them. But we also need to be there to provide a refuge when someone does not have the strength to continue on their way.

We have recently started running a retreat for youth workers on Holy Island. We walked the pilgrim's way, took communion on Cuthbert's island watching the tide carefully so we didn't get cut off, and walked and talked and met with God. Somehow it was easier there, perhaps because, as we called the retreat, we were 'Taking Time and Making Space'. Such prolonged periods of reflection are invaluable on our journey and help us return refreshed, re-envisioned and restored. When asking one of the participants if she planned to come next year her immediate response was, 'Why wouldn't I?'

Music

Music is obviously a significant element for many in their engagement in spiritual practices. This is an approach to using music in prayer:

- Having chosen a piece of music (ask the Holy Spirit to guide you), take a moment of silence and ask God to be present with you as you listen.
- Listen to the piece several times. Take note of any image, phrase, memory, feeling that emerges.
- Settle with something that resonates and offer it to God and ask him to reveal what he is saying to you in it.
- How do you want to respond to what you have experienced? Consider writing, sharing with someone, using art, etc.

- Finish by being still with God and thanking him for what you received (adapted from Blythe, 2006, pp. 52–3).

This is perhaps a more directed version of what is known as 'soaking prayer', which is a spiritual practice being used in some churches today where in essence you rest in God while listening to appropriate music. A friend gave us a soaking song to listen to that talks about God's love and care for us. We have used it ourselves and with many others. People share how hearing the music brings the reality of that love to them in a fresh way and say that it somehow impacts more deeply than just hearing the words. As Sally edited this book she had soaking music on as a background and this helped her feel more peaceful and sensitive to changes that needed to be made.

Theological stories

We live in a world where stories are used to communicate so many things. Parkin notes that 'Their power is in motivating us, stirring up our emotions, stimulating our imagination and making us think and reflect on our own lives' (1998, p. 7). Stories are useful in individual or corporate reflection. These are examples of the range of things we use and have heard others use:

- We were leading a session on praying with the senses and we finished the evening by lighting a sparkler and recalling the Jewish legend that at creation the light was so intense that it shattered into divine sparks which fell to earth and our task is to reveal these sparks through our seeking and service.
- It happened once that Truth walked down the street, as naked as the day he was born. 'A streaker' the people cried and ran into their houses, pulled the blinds and would have nothing to do with him. As Truth walked on alone, wondering why he couldn't get his message across to people, he saw Story approaching him. Story was decked out in fine clothes and bright colours.
  'Why do you go around brooding, Truth?'
  'Because no one accepts me,' responded Truth. 'They run away from me whereas you are always invited into their houses. They love to sit around their fires listening to you. Why does everyone avoid me?'

'It's your nakedness,' replied Story. 'People today find it increasingly difficult to absorb naked truth. Use a little bit of imagination. I'll tell you what . . . I'll lend you some of my fine clothes and you just see how people will take to you.'

Truth followed this advice and decked himself out in Story's bright clothes. People no longer shunned him, they opened their doors to him and since that time Story and Truth have been inseparable companions, respected and loved by all.

- A favourite joke is this: Once a chicken and a pig took a trip together. After many miles and many hours on the road, they got hungry. Finally, the sharp-eyed chicken spotted a restaurant. Approaching the door they read a sign which said, 'Ham and Eggs: Our Speciality!'

'Hold it!' shouted the pig.

'What's the matter?' asked the chicken.

'Plenty. All they want from you is a little compromise. They are asking me for total commitment!'

We have used this for wedding sermons, preaching and teaching but it is also a personal check too – how committed are we?

- This is a story that challenges our tendency to make assumptions and is recounted by Parkin:

This tale goes back to the days – around 40 years ago – when in my home town of Scarborough on the east coast it was a common sight to see knife grinders roaming the streets, and to hear them shouting their wares. 'Knifes to grind . . . any knifes to grind . . .' My mother was used to this practice and was equally used to returning her standard response if the chap came knocking at the door. This was because my father at that time had his own butchery business, where among other things, they had all the equipment necessary for keeping knives constantly sharp, so should any of mother's household utensils become blunt, she would simply hand them over to father who would arrange to have them sharpened. 'No thank you,' was mother's standard reply to the knife grinder 'that won't be necessary', and then by way of explanation, 'my husband does it all'. One day, while at the local shops, my mother had noticed the knife grinder on his rounds and made a mental note to expect a visit later in the day. Sure enough, shortly after her return home, the doorbell rang. Feeling somewhat irritated, as she was in the middle of cooking, mother went to answer the door. 'Yes?'

Without thinking, or even waiting for him to finish, she trotted out her standard line, 'No thank you, my husband does it all . . .' Somewhat perturbed by the look she received as his response, she asked him, 'I'm sorry, what was it you said?' The man replied, 'I said did you want any manure for the garden?'

(1998, pp. 94–5)

- Children's stories are often a profound source of reflection. Take this example from *The Velveteen Rabbit*:

'What is real?' asked the Rabbit one day . . . 'Does it happen all at once like being wound up or bit by bit?' 'It doesn't happen all at once,' said the Skin Horse. 'You become. It takes a long time. That's why it doesn't often happen to people who break easily, or have sharp edges, or have to be carefully kept. Generally, by the time you are Real, most of your hair has been loved off, and your eyes drop out and you get loose in the joints and very shabby. But these things don't matter at all, because once you are Real you can't be ugly, except to people who don't understand.'

(cited in Goldman and Dols, 2006, p. 119)

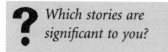 **Which stories are significant to you?**

Thinking back to what our favourite Bible and other stories are can help us understand what has made us who we are. It also helps us to identify the stories that we want to pass on to others.

Takeaways

In church services or other environments such as Lent courses, quiet days or a youth group it can be beneficial to consider if there is something tangible that people can take away. At the bottom of her handbag Sally has a small ceramic star like those she gave to a group of students at their final communion; each time she finds it she is reminded both of the students and of seeing herself positively. Last year our colleague Jo gave us all a clock as part of the term's final service; it is in Sally's eye line when working and she is immediately taken back to that occasion and all those who were present. We have used or experienced being given hearts, baby chicken figures at Easter, confetti doves, flowers, shells, little stones, anything that is practical and where the connection can be easily made.

Processing what has happened to us in the past

One of the discussions we often have as a staff team is how we help people deal with the baggage that holds them back or prevents them from fulfilling their potential. We are all very aware of what some of the things are for us and have looked at getting support and help in different ways. One of the keys in this area is knowing when to get professional or appropriate help but we have found some reflective tools have helped us on the journey of growth, healing and restoration.

Road blocks . . .

One exercise involves drawing a road or roads and adding the road blocks, barriers, boulders and signposts that are or have been there on the journey. We can ask questions such as:

- What are the road blocks that have been placed in our path to slow us down or stop us progressing in our walk with God?
- Have we put anything in the way?
- Do we need to remove or go round anything in the way?
- Can we read the signposts?

Forgiveness

Linked into this is the need to forgive and/or to confess. Augsburger (1996, p. 15) discusses a three-step process that he believes reflects the biblical worldview, which moves from unilateral (on behalf of the offended) to mutual (with both parties involved) forgiveness. How far you get along the process will partly depend on whether the others involved are willing and/or able to engage too. The elements of each stage of the process are summarized below.

Stage 1 Respect and regard

- To see the other as worthful again, in spite of the wrongdoing.
- To see the offence as familiar, in some way similar to one's own shortcomings, and the other as a fellow human being who also needs forgiveness.
- To accept the other as precious and see him/her in equal regard.

Stage 2 Repentance and reconstruction

- To see the offence clearly, feel the injury fully.
- To feel the anger, work through the pain, resolve the demands, release the feelings.
- To hear the other's pain and failure.
- To own one's own part.
- To come to mutual recognition that repentance is genuine.

Stage 3 Reconciliation and relationship

- To reopen the future, to reach out in acceptance.
- To experience healing and new well-being.
- To regain the other as sister or brother.
- To celebrate restored or recreated relationships.

It may be that someone acting as a mediator may be helpful as well if the breakdown in relationship is very serious. Bridge Builders offers training and facilitators to support mediation (see <http://www.menno.org.uk/bridgebuilders>).

Temptations

In ministry it is helpful to have an understanding of which temptations we are vulnerable to. In the Gospel narratives, the first temptation is of the flesh and the question Green asks about Jesus at this point could apply more widely: 'Will Jesus follow the leading of the Spirit and manifest unwavering trust in God to supply his needs; or will he relieve his hunger by exercising his power apart from God?' (1997, p. 194).

The second temptation relates to the way in which humans put something in the place which only God should fill. Each of us is vulnerable to different kinds of idolatry and it is helpful to have people alongside helping and supporting us and challenging us when they see this in us. We need to identify and acknowledge what the potential idols are for us, and work at dealing with them rather than letting them become stumbling blocks to effective ministry.

The third temptation relates to the way in which humans exploit their position or power to achieve their own ends, a perennial issue in ministry. Overall the temptations can be seen as an attempt to deflect Jesus from his purpose as they often are in our own lives. We can ask

? *What temptations are we facing? How are we dealing with them?*

ourselves what the temptations are that may inhibit, mar, detract from or disqualify us from ministry. In a similar vein we may want to ask ourselves: What lies about ourselves do we have or do we listen to and how can we replace these lies with God's word to us and in us.

Other questions we may want to ask ourselves that can relate to issues in our past include:

- Where do we find our worth, identity, purpose and significance? Or where are we tempted to find it?
- What should we be more or less passionate about?
- What should we do more or less of?

For further reflection

Use the following questions to trigger your own reflection:

- Is tolerance enough when relating to those who are different?
- What is praying without ceasing?
- What are the non-negotiables of being a Christian?
- Why is new monasticism popular?

Conclusion

These are only tasters of the spiritual exercises available from the breadth and depth of our faith resources. They may have reminded you of when you have used them in the past or reignited an intention to revisit them. Try them, amend them, just have a go at something you have not used before. Paul still remembers being surprised the first time he went to 'Confession', which was offered during his ordination training. We recommend these exercises to you to keep your walk and times alone with God refreshed and reinvigorated and thus your life and ministry transformed, challenged, encouraged and focused.

? *What new or additional spiritual exercises would facilitate your growth as a reflective minister?*

5

Reframing the past, imagining the future, understanding the present

When your children ask you in time to come, 'What is the mean-
ing of the decrees and the statutes and the ordinances that the
LORD our God has commanded you? then you shall say to your
children . . .   *(Deuteronomy 6.20–21a)*

The envisioning of an alternative future . . . creates a critical per-
spective from which the oppressive structures of the present can
be changed.   *(Sally McFague)*

Our Christian story is rich with resources for reflection and we do
well to take note of the past to avoid history repeating itself. The word
'tradition' is sometimes used by theologians to encompass historical
sources and insights. As McGrath suggests, 'The word "Tradition"
implies not merely something that is handed down, but an active
process of reflection by which theological or spiritual insights are
valued, assessed, and transmitted from one generation to another'
(1994, p. 188). There are dangers with the word and an immediate
reaction to hearing it can be negative as some think it means being
tied and limited to the practices of the past. We prefer the more
dynamic approach that McGrath's quote implies.

Reframing and rewriting classic texts

One of the most stimulating ways we have used our Christian heritage is to rewrite classic texts for our current contexts. We have used
this idea in various groups and find that this gives a creative format
to work with. We have used this tool to help people develop a
theology of ministry, church mission statements and to articulate
personal calling, value, passion and vision, for example. The benefit
of this approach is that we do not have to start from scratch and can

work with something already written rather than start with a blank sheet of paper. Often the hardest part of doing a piece of work is coming up with the original idea and this approach gives somewhere to build from.

Examples of classic texts

I have a dream . . . Martin Luther King

> I have a dream that one day this nation will rise up and live out the true meaning of its creed: 'We hold these truths to be self-evident: that all men are created equal.' I have a dream that one day on the red hills of Georgia the sons of former slaves and the sons of former slave owners will be able to sit down together at the table of brotherhood . . . I have a dream that my four little children will one day live in a nation where they will not be judged by the color of their skin but by the content of their character . . . I have a dream today. I have a dream that one day every valley shall be exalted, every hill and mountain shall be made low, the rough places will be made plain, and the crooked places will be made straight, and the glory of the Lord shall be revealed, and all flesh shall see it together . . . When we allow freedom to ring, when we let it ring from every village and every hamlet, from every state and every city, we will be able to speed up that day when all of God's children, black men and white men, Jews and Gentiles, Protestants and Catholics, will be able to join hands and sing in the words of the old Negro spiritual, 'Free at last! free at last! thank God Almighty, we are free at last!'
>
> (Extracts from the speech given on 28 August 1963 in Washington, DC <http://www.usconstitution.net/dream.html>)

This speech is seen by some as the pinnacle of the Civil Rights movement in the USA in the 1960s. The speech was the culmination of a protest march about the segregation and persecution of black people in the USA, especially the southern states where separate restaurants, toilets, drinking fountains and bus seats, for example, were common experiences for black people. It must be one of the world's most well-known speeches and inspired not only the black community but other communities in the world. Paul has used this for years to encourage youth workers to articulate their own dreams for the young people they work with.

We like the idea of dream, it puts our desires and perhaps frustrations in our ministries into a future orientation. It takes it past today or even tomorrow and voices our hopes and aspirations for our world, people groups or communities. This is an example from one of those youth workers, Steve Hirst, who was working in Birmingham when he wrote this:

> I have a dream . . . that we can live in a world, a community, that is free from oppression, deprivation and marginalization. The hungry fed, the hopeless with a future, the rejected empowered. Where race, gender, age, background, faith and financial status doesn't bring division, separation and prejudice. Maybe then we will genuinely understand the concept of 'shalom', in its holistic sense, and see the kingdom of God on earth, as it is in heaven!

As you can see from this example it provides a creative way of articulating hopes and aspirations. It honours and connects us to an important movement and links this tradition to our own day and culture. It also introduces us to the idea of contextual theologies, in this case black but it might be liberation, feminist, green, etc. The very premise of contextual theology relates to our values and the purpose of this book, in that it desires to take seriously the experiences and location of God's people today as well as in the past. When doing an exercise like this with a group it can be helpful to ask questions such as:

- What issues are important to us today?
- What are the theological perspectives on this issue?
- How might the issue be addressed?
- What is a creative way of presenting the issue and a challenge to address it?

First they came . . . by Martin Niemöller

Martin Niemöller is best known as a pastor in Nazi Germany in the 1930s and 1940s. Although he fought in the First World War he became an outspoken critic of the Nazi regime. He said this in response to a student's question, 'How could it happen?'

> First they came for the Communists, but I was not a Communist so I did not speak out. Then they came for the Socialists and the Trade Unionists, but I was neither, so I did not speak out. Then they came for the Jews, but I was not a Jew so I did not speak out. And when they came for me, there was no one left to speak out for me.
>
> (http://www.blacktriangle.org/blog/?p=1104)

93

What we like about this text is that it encourages us to reflect on the temptations we face, or have faced, and to be honest in our articulation of them. It also leads us to think about who are the marginalized in our communities and perhaps encourages us to be advocates for them. In doing a search about this text, one of the results we found contained the statement, 'Let's not have Martin Niemöller's regrets' in relation to the execution of two young men for being gay.

> **?** *Who do we need to advocate for or help to advocate on their own behalf?*

Such exercises can also be useful to introduce the thoughts of our favourite writers to others and to help us draw out meanings and applications for our own context. We find Henri Nouwen a constant source of inspirational insights. Joyce Rupp, Kathleen Norris and Dorothy Day are others we draw on from outside our own tradition.

> **?** *Which inspirational passage would be helpful to reframe for your context?*

Creeds and affirmations of faith

Creeds are another rich source for reflection. Many have rewritten creeds for their own context, taking as models the statements of faith made by early Christians and reframing them. We are not suggesting changing the doctrine of the original creeds, rather, finding new ways of speaking about the Trinitarian God. There are many groups and people developing creative liturgy, this is an example from the Iona Community <www.iona.org.uk>. We like the direct challenge of this one:

> **?** *In what ways would you reframe a creed or affirmation of faith in language that would resonate with those you work or worship with?*

> We believe that God is present in the darkness before dawn; in the waiting and uncertainty where fear and courage join hands, conflict and caring link arms and the sun rises over the barbed wire.

We believe in a with-us God who sits down in our midst to share our humanity.

We affirm a faith that takes us beyond the safe place: into action, into vulnerability and into the streets.

We commit ourselves to work for change and put ourselves on the line; to bear responsibility, take risks, live powerfully and face humiliation; to stand with those on the edge, to choose life and be used by the Spirit for God's new community of hope. Amen.

(Wild Goose Worship Group, 2001, p. 109)

Biblical resources and starting points

Different Bible translations will tend to suit different contexts and situations. For example, Sally prefers the NRSV for its inclusive language but will often use *The Message* if reading a familiar passage with long-time Christians because the different language and concepts help the meaning to be heard afresh. Again, we tend to take the original text and then ask people to use it as a springboard for reflection. For example, we would read Luke 4.18–21 and ask questions such as:

• Where is the Spirit of the Lord upon us?
• What has God called us to do?
• What has the Lord anointed us for?

Answers to these questions can be sought individually or corporately. When doing this exercise, Paul responds that the Lord has anointed him to pastor those in pain, help people fulfil their potential and communicate God's love so people know that they are loved by God.

Something similar can be done with the Great Commission, Matthew 28.18–20.

• What does it mean for us to go and make disciples?
• What has God instructed us to 'make'?

The Northumbria Community <www.northumbriacommunity.org> seeks to respond afresh to Scripture-based questions such as, 'How shall we sing the Lord's song in a strange land?' (Psalm 137.4) and their Morning Prayer liturgy asks if we love God with all our heart, soul, mind and strength (from Mark 12.28–31, *Celtic Daily Prayer*, 2000, p. 17).

Ten commandments

While he was Chair of the National Youth Agency, Bishop Roger Sainsbury reframed the ten commandments for youth work. While some may want to debate the content they provide a starting point for discussing how we should work with young people today:

1 Listen to the voices of young people.
2 Have a special concern for the socially excluded and disadvantaged.
3 Work co-operatively with other agencies, particularly schools.
4 Give spiritual development a priority.
5 Demonstrate tough love.
6 Offer emotional and spiritual security.
7 Organize activities that help young people feel valued and significant.
8 Challenge the demonization of young people.
9 Help build community cohesion by youth work that educates young people to value our common humanity and shared citizenship, not sectarian hate.
10 Be active politically to seek long-term funding for youth work from national and local government.

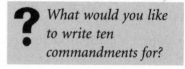 *What would you like to write ten commandments for?*

Responses

There are many ways of helping people to reflect on the Bible, one being to ask for a physical, rather than just a verbal, response. Matthew 11.28 encourages those of us who are weary and heavy-laden to come to Jesus. When leading a service on this theme we had a pile of stones and invited people to come forward, take a stone and place it by the cross to signify that they were leaving their burden with Jesus. We have developed this reflective exercise in our chapel at the Children's Hospital in Birmingham. In front of the altar there is a large wooden plate full of stones. Children, their families and staff are invited to take a stone from the tray and leave it on the altar. We connect this to 1 Peter 5.7 where we are encouraged to 'Cast all your anxiety on him, because he cares for you'. We occasionally use this reflection as a part of our weekly staff prayers at the hospital and afterwards Paul usually carries a small stone around in his pocket for a week or so. He finds it helpful as a reminder of the pressures on families, how heavy the weight of their children's illness must be on them, how God wishes to help them carry their load and what small part he might be privileged to play as he obeys the injunction to bear one another's burdens (Galatians 6.2).

Top ten Scriptures

When we were young, highlights of the week included listening to the charts on the radio and watching *Top of the Pops*. Who was in and out of the top ten was a big deal. We've been encouraged to think of how the concept of a 'top ten' might help aid reflection. One idea we've found beneficial is to identify our top ten scriptures. It helps us see what has shaped us theologically or how our values shape our approach to theology – it is one of those chicken-and-egg discussions where we sometimes can't tell which is primary. This is a list for an urban youth worker:

- Psalm 121 – our help comes from the Lord
- Proverbs 3.5–8 – trust in the Lord with all your heart
- Isaiah 43.1–4 – God is with us whatever the circumstances
- Micah 6.8 – justice, mercy and humility
- Matthew 25.31–46 – parable of the sheep and goats
- Luke 10.17–20 – rejoice your names are written in heaven
- Luke 19.41 – Jesus weeps over Jerusalem
- Romans 8.28 – God works things out for good
- Ephesians 4.11–15 – equipping the saints for works of service
- Philippians 2.5–11 – let the same mind be in you as in Jesus

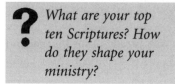

What are your top ten Scriptures? How do they shape your ministry?

Looking over such a list helps us see where we have come from in our faith journey, helps us assess what is important to us now and gives insight for the future too.

Other top tens

The idea of a 'top ten' can be used for other lists as well. For example, you could think of the top ten books that have shaped your life and ministry. Our lists are reproduced below. The entries might not have been chosen for the reason you think and reflect both secular and Christian titles. They are in alphabetical order of author rather than influence.

Paul's

- *Dibs in Search of Self*, Virginia Axline
- *The Cost of Discipleship*, Dietrich Bonhoeffer
- *The Practice of the Presence of God*, Brother Lawrence
- *The 7 Habits of Highly Effective People*, Stephen Covey
- *Sleeping with Bread*, Dennis Linn, Sheila Fabricant Linn, Matthew Linn
- *Jesus: A Gospel*, Henri Nouwen
- *Holiness*, J. C. Ryle
- *Spiritual Leadership*, J. Oswald Sanders
- *One Day in the Life of Ivan Denisovich*, Aleksandr Solzhenitsyn
- *The Shack*, Wm Paul Young

Sally's

- *Little Women*, Louisa M. Alcott
- *Jonathan Livingston Seagull*, Richard Bach
- *Nine O'Clock in the Morning*, Dennis Bennett
- *Kids at the Door*, Bob Holman
- *Soul Friend*, Kenneth Leech
- *Sleeping with Bread*, Dennis Linn, Sheila Fabricant Linn, Matthew Linn
- *Reaching Out*, Henri Nouwen
- *Fat is a Feminist Issue*, Susie Orbach
- *Dear Heart, Come Home*, Joyce Rupp
- *Why Settle for More and Miss the Best?* Tom Sine

There are very good reasons for our choices and we can argue theologically even for those books that we were told were 'dodgy' when we were younger! Paul's list of books was already in his journal and was the product of a period of time. Sally's was sparked off by Paul's and was completed in an evening.

In some ways such exercises are quite difficult to do but are worth devoting time to as they can help crystallize our thinking, possibly help us see where we may have drifted from our early passions (which may be right but could be distractions). They can also be significant ways of passing on some of our experience. As leaders we may want to use such material in mentoring or in encouraging others. Over the years we have bought multiple copies of some books and given them away or loaned them to others we think would enjoy them too. We have also benefited from others doing this for us. Several of the books on Paul's list have either been recommended or lent to him.

What are your top ten books? Can you track their influence?

The most recent was when someone at work lent Paul a copy of *The Shack*. She had underlined many passages that had an impact on her and this was a bonus to be gained from reading such a wonderful book.

Other ideas would be top ten songs or films that have influenced you.

Reflecting with theology

Robin Greenwood has a premise that if you want to know what a priest should do then you need to know what the Church should do and if you want to know what the Church should do then you need to find out what God is like (1994, p. 180). Paul's first response to the question, 'What is God like?' is that he is Trinitarian, so in thinking about ministry he begins by looking at the Trinity. This is a challenge we present to our students too. We have a wide range of Trinity (or at least three-figured) statues with different sized and gendered people.

What are the key theological questions you wish to ask yourself and for what area of ministry?

Really being honest about how we see and respond to the Trinity can give insight into our beliefs and actions in our ministry. One of the things we have speculated on is: if you drew the Trinity as a pie chart would there be three equal pieces or is our construction of the Trinity weighted more towards one person than the other two?

In working with students we encourage them to ask questions that help them connect theology to their ministry. Key questions are:

- How is the nature and function of the Trinity reflected in our practice?
- Where is salvation in our work?

- How are the Christ roles worked out?
- Where is the kingdom of God reflected in this context?
- Where and how do we see the image of God in our context?
- Where is God already at work (*missio dei*)?

Learning from monastic communities

We have mixed feelings about the concept of rule and rhythm of life. While the model is beneficial, the words are not helpful, particularly the word rule, which may have etymological roots in measurement, but sounds like legalism. Earlier we talked about spending time on Holy Island and it was one occasion we were there that we decided instead of using the words rule and rhythm to change this to marker posts and shelters. Thus we have marker posts on a daily, weekly, monthly, periodic and annual basis that help to keep us on track and we have shelters that are people, places and practices where we can go to recharge, refresh and recreate. Sally offers a model for developing this in *Sustaining Your Spirituality* (Nash, 2006).

The traditional monastic vows of poverty, chastity and obedience are terms that don't always resonate in our current cultural environment. Communities that are sometimes known as the new monastic movements have often reframed them. The Northumbria Community has adopted availability and vulnerability, which are just as challenging when you begin to think what they may mean when you live them out in practice. The Community of Aidan and Hilda <www.aidanandhilda.org.uk> use the terms simplicity and purity along with obedience and in their explanation of them locate obedience in the understanding of the Body of Christ (1 Corinthians 12).

Paul has been influenced by the attitude of Brother Lawrence who practised the presence of God in whatever he did, whether washing up or being in the garden. This has helped Paul have a positive attitude towards all the less glamorous things that go with being in ministry and to see a servant heart as something that should underpin what we do. He still remembers the surprise he felt when the person who headed up the Christian organization we worked for asked him to move some chairs and said that he had been looking for someone who he thought he could ask to do such a job. We would expect anyone in ministry to be willing to do the mundane as well as the more glamorous tasks.

For further reflection

Use the following to trigger your own reflection:

- What does it mean to be made in the image of God?
- 'We are fighting Germany, we are fighting Austria, we are fighting drink. And as far as I can see the greatest of these deadliest foes is drink' (Lloyd George, 1914).
- Rewrite a folk story, legend or classical text for today.
- The last Morse code message was sent in 1997: 'Calling all. This is our last cry before our eternal silence.'

Paradigm shifts

Another list that has helped Paul reflect on his Christian and ministerial journey is his key paradigm shifts. These are both experiences that taught him something and insights that changed him. Significant ones include the following:

- Feeling like he was loved into the kingdom at Grays Baptist Church (rather than being convinced by apologetics).
- Being top student at catering college and feeling that he had succeeded at something for the first time and now had a sense of purpose for the future, even though that changed after four years working as a chef.
- Being 'got' by the Holy Spirit after joining Youth for Christ as a volunteer and getting the charismatic language to go with some of the things he had previously experienced.
- Having a fantastic year as a volunteer team leader and then an awful one, and learning that one leadership style doesn't fit everyone or everywhere!
- Understanding that women are equal and can have the same roles in ministry as men – a shift that needed to happen to be able to marry Sally!
- At the end of the day as part of his quiet/reflection time Paul sometimes waters the plants in our prayer room. In doing this he noticed that some plants need more water than others or need watering more or less often. If you try to water a dry plant quickly the water just pours out the bottom, but if you pour it in very

slowly the soil has a chance to absorb the moisture. This has been a helpful thought both personally for different times of life but also in working with individuals in ministry.

- On a trip to Israel we were by the Sea of Galilee and the song 'To be in your presence' came into Paul's mind and he felt God saying to him clearly that what was important was to be in the presence of God, not being in ministry or anything else but being with God. It helps get things into proportion when God speaks to us like that.

- A recent insight is from Paul's car journey to the hospital. He noticed that if he exercised grace and let people out at junctions and didn't drive aggressively then he felt better and other people often acted more graciously to him too. It helped him think about what whole-life witnessing means and is an everyday way of doing random acts of kindness in a context where they don't happen very often as everyone thinks of themselves and their journeys.

- Being loved by Sally has been influential but also the realization that Sally needs to be loved in the way that she wants, not the way Paul thinks. The cup of tea early in the morning is still one of those sticking points!

What are the significant paradigm shifts in your life? Why and how did they happen and what effect have they had on you?

Conclusion

One of the main reasons why we are passionate about these types of tools for reflection is not just the creativity of the outcome but the access they give us and those we work with to the rich heritage we have in our Christian

What tool or exercise would help you draw together and articulate your priorities for your ministry?

faith. They can help us see the past differently, re-imagine the future and live differently in today.

6

Using culture in reflection

A culture may be conceived as a network of beliefs and purposes
in which any string in the net pulls and is pulled by the others,
thus perpetually changing the configuration of the whole.

(Jacques Barzun)

To read the signs of the times, to hear the voices of the age – these
evocative images challenge the community of faith to strengthen
its dialogue with the culture in which it lives.

(James D. Whitehead and Evelyn Eaton Whitehead)

If we believe that this is God's world, and God is at work in it
(the missio dei*), and if we further accept the most obvious con-*
sequences of this belief – that there can be no cultural no-go areas
from God – then this must mean God can be found even, maybe
especially, in the midst of all our struggles to be fully human.

(John Drane)

We are immersed in culture. It influences every area of our lives. In
ministry we cannot avoid reflecting on culture as it impacts all that
we do. The sermon we preach at church is crafted for a time, people
and place. That we live in Birmingham, a multicultural and multi-
faith city, cannot help but shape the way we see our faith and
ministry. In this chapter we mainly focus on reflecting on popular
culture. However, there is a significant body of work that explores
the connectedness between theology and culture from a range of perspectives and to grasp the breadth of the debate you may want to read
some of the books listed in the further readings for this chapter.

Mahan offers this reflection, which summarizes our perspective in
including this chapter in the book, although in many ways it has been
the most difficult to write because of the tensions inherent in what
is a growing field:

[we] must ourselves embody religion in mass mediated culture and bear witness to the sacred in the midst of a society shaped by the values of consumption. We are not separate from that culture. With everyone else, we participate in it, view our lives through the lens of the media, and participate in the process of creating meaning from the complex of symbols and rituals available to us.   (2007, p. 61)

Authors suggest a variety of different ways of relating Christian faith and culture. Often quoted is that of Niebuhr (1951) who identified five such categories:

- Christ against culture
- the Christ of culture
- Christ above culture
- Christ and culture in paradox
- Christ the transformer of culture.

At a simple level, and in some ways how we may operate in practice, we see three approaches:

- Christianity and Christians challenge culture (e.g. Oscar Romero, Martin Luther King, Dorothy Day, Mother Teresa, Make Poverty History).
- Christianity and Christians are challenged by culture (e.g. women's movement, environmental lobby).
- Christianity and Christians use the resources of culture in the pursuit of mission (Alpha, sports outreach).

Different Christian traditions choose which of these perspectives to follow and some of the debates in Christianity partly have their roots in the understanding of culture that has been adopted. Percy nuances this understanding and suggests that in the last 50 years there have been two main approaches to engaging with contemporary culture. 'The first broadly conceives of the engagement as a form of interlocking combative encounter with contemporary culture' (2005, p. 63), which is probably the tradition both of us grew up with. Sally, for example, remembers her church picketing the cinema showing *The Exorcist*. 'The second broadly sees it as a form of intrarelated binding, covenant or commitment' (Percy, 2005, p. 63). This is where we see ourselves now although occasionally we see or hear something that makes us think we still have sympathy with the first approach! Perhaps our tradition still has an impact on us as also does our belief that the exhortation to the Philippians (4.8) to think on things that are lovely and admirable is a beneficial one. In lecturing on the Christian priest today, Rowan Williams has this advice:

> This 'seeing', then, has to involve a fair bit of literacy about the world we're in – literacy about our culture (cultures, rather), about how our contemporary emotions and myths work, about the human heart. The priest's obligation to maintain such literacy is not just to do with the need to speak to people in the language they understand, in a missionary context; it is grounded in the need to show believers the world they live in and help them to respond not instantly or shallowly but with truthfulness and discernment. There has to be in every priest just a bit of the poet and artist – enough to keep alive a distaste for nonsense, cheapness of words and ideas, stale and predictable reactions.
>
> (2004)

We have no choice but to engage critically with culture. Part of this will involve engagement in a broader range of disciplines than just theology. Insights from social science are now commonly used in conversation with theology to reflect and explore ministry (e.g. Watts, 2002; Gill, 1996) and cross-disciplinary teams are involved in researching from different perspectives (e.g. Savage *et al.*, 2006).

? *How do you view and treat culture – challenge, challenged by or make use of?*

Context

We might read our Bibles for a few minutes a day; most of the rest of the time we are surrounded by cultural texts that speak to us at the conscious and subconscious levels. In much of what we see, read, watch or listen to there is some sort of embedded or implicit theology which can influence us. Value-neutral media doesn't exist and we always take with us our own preconceptions, assumptions and theological perspectives. There is likely to be a belief system underpinning any piece of media and trying to uncover this helps us to be more aware of how we may be influenced by it. Wanting to engage with contemporary culture, however, doesn't mean a dismissal of the Bible if that is an important tool for you. Drane tells how he has always been interested in the contemporary relevance of the Bible but when

For further reflection

These are all from our mass media consumption (we don't necessarily agree with them!), but use any you find helpful to trigger your own reflection:

- What is the appeal of being a football fan?
- Come for the price, stay for the advice (health food shop).
- If everything is marriage, then marriage is nothing.
- People's focus of hope has moved from Sunday morning to Saturday night.
- Mild depression is the new norm.
- Doing nothing is the new busy.
- Hate something, change something, make something better (car advert).
- If you want to be happy take a pill, if you want to be right face the truth.

considering the cultural challenges faced by the Church, his understanding is filtered through insights from Scripture and tradition (2008, p. 1). Such reflection has led him to identify four key everyday experiences that the Church needs to take seriously in the current cultural context and may be significant in any thoughts we have about ministry:

- Everyday life presents us with the realization that nothing seems to work the way it once did.
- The way Western people have lived is not the only possible way to be, nor is it the only way that looks as if it might lead to a fulfilled and meaningful life.
- There is a frequently expressed desire to be 'spiritual' rather than religious.
- There is a consciousness that we live in fearful times (2008, pp. 11–16).

If we reflect on our local context we may have other elements we want to add. Owen works in a community with identity issues that have arisen because of local political decisions about where to build a ring road. The people on the 'wrong' side of the road have a sense

? *What is the cultural context of your community and how does this impact reflection?*

of isolation and abandonment as an underpinning narrative to their lives, as now accessing the local shops is much more complex and some of the houses were cleared to make the road possible. Those on the other side of the road seem to be more advantaged and houses there are more sought after. Knowing the history can help us understand the culture we are trying to minister in.

Celtic spirituality

A part of the contemporary church culture we are connected to is Celtic spirituality. In our links with the Northumbria Community and the Community of Aidan and Hilda we have predominantly encountered those who minister in other parts of the Church but who find in their association with the communities a nurturing of their spirituality and faith. One of the characteristics of Celtic values is a sympathetic attitude towards the surrounding culture, perhaps because of an understanding of the roots of the early expressions of the Celtic church in Britain, where local holy places were not burnt or destroyed but claimed and renamed into the new religion. Celtic celebrations, wells, seasons and standing stones were adopted by Christians. This we understand enabled local indigenous communities to become Christian while not betraying all they had been. The Celtic church was culture friendly (Simpson and Lyons Lee, 2008, pp. 36f.). The Northumbria Community talks about the 'heretical imperative' (a term associated with Peter Berger), which means: 'to choose to seek God in Christ and to discover His Truth in a pluralistic, secular and materialistic world, being unafraid to listen or to ask awkward questions, of others and ourselves, as part of the quest' <http://northumbriacommunity.org>. In a booklet on this topic, Trevor Miller offers some guidelines which have helped us in our reflections on contemporary culture as it gives some boundaries to reflect within:

- We must emphasize strong convictions not dead certainties.
- We must seek to keep the questions alive.
- We must learn to share points of connectedness.

- We must endeavour to put relationship above reputation.
- We must strive to live vocationally (2003, pp. 27–35).

Groups such as the Northumbria Community have led us to aspects of a different spiritual culture from our evangelical heritage, and this has enriched and broadened our experience. Sadly we both grew up with the idea that Catholics were not real Christians and ironically now many of our significant influences and sacred places are Roman Catholic. Prejudicial attitudes towards other cultures and cultural manifestations cause much conflict and grief and it is good to look at where our culture adopts a wrong attitude to someone or something different.

Images and imagination

We are bombarded with images but it is our imagination that helps us make the leap between an image and the meaning it has for us. Arthur suggests that there is a lack of imagination among (young) people today in relation to the claims of the gospel and that to communicate effectively we need to help people develop their imaginations (2007, p. 29). Imagination can be defined as 'the image-making facility of the intellect that helps us discover, process, and creatively express coherent meaning . . . it's how we make connections between thought and experience, word and image, self and other, seen and unseen' (Arthur, 2007, p. 53). We need imagination to engage with stories, in essence to engage with the many popular culture products that we encounter today. Many of the exercises in this book help us develop our imaginations.

Metaphors of culture

Although some of these perhaps belong in the chapter on metaphor we wanted to list here some of the ways of seeing culture (or facets of culture) we have used, found helpful or learnt from students:

? *Which metaphors of culture resonate? How does this impact or influence your ministry?*

Tsunami, catalyst, conception, GPS, mini me, evolution, invisible, capsize, magnet, drowning, rescue, game, dream, masks, gagged, treasure, open door, healing, journey, rechargeable batteries, aeration, divorce, pasture, blinkers, filter, playground, iceberg, paradise, lens/glasses, building blocks, garden, transmitter, turn the light on, wake up and smell the coffee, drinking from other wells, short shelf life.

Analysing texts from popular culture

We both grew up with popular music providing a background to all we did. Occasionally we have been made to feel inferior for knowing little about more highbrow culture. Marsh offers a strong apologetic for engaging with popular culture (specifically film in this instance) and suggests that doctrines of creation, incarnation and the Spirit provide a rationale for engaging with and respecting a range of human artistic endeavour while acknowledging that not all products are 'equally valid or equally revelatory work of God' (2004, p. 144). Here we are using the term 'cultural text' to apply to any media: song, book, play, picture, etc. Ward has taken models from cultural and media studies and suggests that 'texts' can be read through

- production, representation, consumption (cultural studies) and
- institution, text, audience (media studies) (2008, p. 82).

This means paying attention to how, where, why and who a text was created by, what form it is in and what this means in the context, as well as issues around who is reading the text, how they understand it and what impact it has on the way it is heard. Some useful questions to help us reflect on texts include:

- What genre is it and what are the implications of that?
- What other texts does it remind you of?
- What was happening in the world when it was created?
- Who is the target audience? Why do you think that?
- What is the ultimate concern here?
- Is there genuine perspective?
- Is anyone being left out? What perspective would they bring?
- How does our experience and understanding of God answer questions raised by the text's ultimate concern? What does our faith tradition say?

- In what way does the text support or undermine our faith and beliefs?
- Be aware of feelings. What surprises, moves, disturbs, challenges, excites . . . ?
- What are your final reflections? (adapted from Blythe, 2006, pp. 108–9).

This can be used or adapted for a range of media and can be useful for group discussions. For a good range of resources to help in thinking critically about contemporary popular culture, see <www.damaris.org> or <www.licc.org.uk>. If using such resources in a group context then be aware of copyright restrictions on some media (see <www.copyrightservice.co.uk> for some basic information).

Reflecting with music

Music is a significant influence in the lives of many. As Sally was driving to order a cake for church, the song 'American Pie' came on the radio. Immediately she was transported back to her teenage years and the earnest discussions about the imagery and symbolism in the song – when was the day the music died? Music is a powerful medium which can be used in a range of ways. There is a song called 'Fix you' by Coldplay. Listening to it, Paul realized why he is tempted to try to fix people and relationships. He reflects:

> You know sometimes you hear something that just rings true and I used this interjection into my comfortable world to challenge and sharpen my practice and values. What is it about me that wants to fix people? Why do I think they are broken? Being reflective has many benefits and virtues but being honest is high up on the list. Using this song facilitated me in some honest reflection on how and why I am in ministry and the temptations that I could buy into should I not be living in a place of self-understanding and reflective practice. I also had to ask myself the question: 'Do I think I am broke and in need of fixing and would like someone to come and save me? If I am really honest there are times when I may act in a way with Sally that encourages this. I understand that others have used this song to illustrate what God desires for humanity. It is interesting to me that this is not what I thought of when I first heard the song, but this illustrates how the same starting point leads to different outcomes.

Another aspect of music that is important to reflect on is the worship songs we sing (see Ward, 2005, for an in-depth treatment of this topic). Some observe that our beliefs and theology may be shaped more by what we sing than by the teaching that we hear and that there may be times we can't recall if something is a song lyric or a verse from the Bible. Because of the power of music, and the number of times that we may sing many songs (in some traditions), they can get into our subconscious. For those of us who choose what is sung in church or other contexts it may be worth reflecting on what theology is being communicated through what is sung and on whether this complements or is dissonant with what is being preached, taught or communicated in other ways.

'Musicals'

One of the ways we use music in a variety of teaching contexts is encouraging people to develop 'musicals'. Paul was doing a chaplaincy qualification and the class was given an assignment which resulted in his compiling 'Chaplaincy – the Musical', which was a selection of songs that connected with all the different aspects of his pastoral work with children, their families and staff and their hopes, fears, pressures and aspirations. In presenting the piece of work Paul talked about who might request each song and why and played short clips from his compilation, which included 'Where is the love?' (Black-eyed Peas), 'Candle in the wind' (Diana version by Elton John), 'Tears from heaven' (Eric Clapton), and 'I'll be missing you' (Puff Daddy). At the end of his presentation there was a deadly hush in the classroom. A first thought was that people were bored or asleep but feedback suggested that the songs had had a profound impact on those who were listening. A couple of years later Paul met one of these students and this was her memory of Paul. Subsequently Paul has reflected on the task and realized that he both thought of songs that resonated with aspects of his work and also, as he was going through his CDs, was inspired by what he listened to and made connections and insights from the songs. The process of making such choices can be very insightful as we recognize what it is about us or a particular song that is so significant.

> **?** *Is there a 'musical' you could or should make to bring insight to a facet of ministry?*

Reflecting with film

We have had students complain that going to the cinema is no longer a leisure activity as now they see everything through the lens of theological reflection. Browne comments that 'Film shows us ourselves, and is a mirror both of our achievements and of our strivings; we make meaning in all we do, whether this is done in order to illuminate our path or to search for the infinite' (1997, p. 19). Saturday night is film night in our house and Paul would say that he has learnt from films in the same way as from books. Films such as *Braveheart, Crimson Tide, Patton, We Were Soldiers* and *Coach Carter* have helped him reflect on his own leadership style, along with television shows such as *West Wing* and *Band of Brothers*. A line from *Along Came a Spider*, that suggests we do what we are, brought new insight into vocation. What is it we cannot help doing (in a positive ministry sense)? What does that say about us and what God has called us to?

When teaching how to write reflective journals Sally likes to use 'Summer nights' from *Grease* to help students understand that we need to identify the perspective from which we are telling the story and be aware that others see things differently from us. The end of *Grease*, where both Sandy and Danny appear with a new image, helps us to reflect on identity and finding our authentic self rather than becoming who others want us to be – even if in the short term it appears to be happy ever after! Or perhaps they return to the Sandy and Danny who originally met on a beach and were not being conformed to the image their peers had for them.

Paul uses the scene from *The Green Mile*, where the prisoner heals the prison guard, as part of a discussion on salvation or our need to be open to learning from those we work among as well as expecting that they may learn from us.

Selina used a scene in *Talladega Nights* where grace is being said and the character prays to 'baby Jesus'. It is a fascinating insight into the people's constructs of Jesus and provides a starting place for a discussion on Christology and a realization that the word 'Jesus' is open to so many interpretations.

However, we need to realize that what we watch may shape us negatively as well. MacDonald argues that:

> films have a habit of slipping under the guard of our convictions and taking possession of our emotional sympathies. In suspending our

normal judgements about what is plausible we can also jettison our
beliefs about what is right and wrong ... but is it possible that an experience that sometimes moves us to anger, triumph, tears or laughter does
not take any root in our subconscious attitudes?   (1991, p. 15)

While there are claims that the evidence is ambiguous, there are
significant academic studies that suggest that violence on screen can
have a range of negative influences on behaviour, for example:

imitation of violent roles and acts of aggression, triggering aggres-
sive impulses in predisposed individuals, desensitizing feelings of
sympathy towards victims, creating an indifference to the use of violence, and creating a frame of mind that sees violent acts as a socially
acceptable response to stress and frustration.

(Pennell and Browne, 1999)

This should encourage us to help people develop critical skills in
examining their use of media. Marsh, as part of a strong plea for film-
watching as spiritual practice and theological enterprise, argues that
'attention to film and the practice of film-watching accentuates these
mutually critical aspects of theology's task: how cultures critique
theologies and how theologies critique cultures' (2004, pp. 146–7).

It is not just films but such media as television programmes,
advertisements and pop videos that can speak to us significantly.
While writing this Paul was very taken by an advert for Oxfam
where a cartoon communicates the concept of no injustice. Previously he liked the car advert where people's lives became colourful
while the car was around but when it wasn't there they were walking glumly along the road. Good sources of such material are
<www.youtube.com> and <www.wingclips.com>. Petra used the
advert for a drink which refreshes the parts other drinks can't reach
as a way of talking about the Holy Spirit and God's capacity to impact
every part of our lives if we choose to let him.

Stories

In his early Christian life, Paul was not too keen on stories unless
they were biblical or Christian testimonies, part of an attitude to wider
culture he perhaps imbibed. However, now he loves stories and on
leaving his first parish gave everyone at the final service a booklet of
his favourites. These included:

As the old man walked along the beach, he noticed a young woman ahead of him picking up starfish and flinging them into the sea. Finally catching up with the young woman, he asked her why she was doing this. The answer was that the stranded starfish would die if left until the morning.

'But the beach goes on for miles and there are hundreds of starfish', countered the other. 'How can you make any difference?'

The young woman looked at the starfish in her hand and threw it safely in the waves. 'It will make a difference to this one,' she said. (There are lots of versions of this online; we first heard it from Mike Riddell.)

Paul has always believed this as a principle but this story has had an impact that has shaped the way he ministers, the values he has and the way he sees people. His work at the hospital can sometimes be very unpredictable. His team have an open-door policy for both families and staff and you never quite know what the next knock on the door or bleep of the pager might bring and, as the saying goes, 'You cannot change the world for everybody but you can change one person's world.'

Why do stories work? Arthur suggests it is because:

through its basic ingredients (character, plot, setting, tone) story provides a satisfying pattern for the imagination to grab hold of. And through its thematic structure (form), story incarnates meaning, embodies content, rather than confronting the hearer's reason with propositional argument. It presents itself in nonthreatening ways so the hearer's defences are down; it slips past those 'watchful dragons' and makes connections that are not easily forgotten.   (2007, p. 82)

She notes that story helps people engage with such issues or concepts as intimacy, identity, wonder, world building, play, timelessness, enchantment, resonance, subversion and mystery (Arthur, 2007, pp. 83–7). We live in a narrative-oriented world and need to become fluent in telling and interpreting stories (see pp. 85–7 for more about truth and story). The great thing about stories is that they need no explanation. We like the way we can sit with a story, just listen to it, replay it in our mind, to hear or see something else and receive fresh insight.

Consider too real-life stories. Sally uses a film about the life of Dietrich Bonhoeffer (*Agent of Grace*) to teach something of his theology, or the *Rosa Parks Story* to communicate something about the injustice faced by minority groups. Testimonies too are really powerful; hearing how God has worked in the life of someone like us somehow helps us have faith that God will work in our lives too. Stories relate, are interesting, engage, are memorable and versatile and are a fruitful tool for reflection.

Sayings

There is a well-known proverb: 'Give a person a fish and you feed them for a day. Teach a person to fish and you feed them for life.' We have always liked this proverb as it connects with our values and principles of ministry, of empowerment and facilitation rather than doing everything for someone. However, we recently realized that we had not got the most out of this proverb. Shane Claiborne critiques it for not going far enough: 'We are about ending poverty, not simply managing it. We give people fish. We teach them to fish. We tear down walls that have been built up around the fish pond. And we figure out who polluted it' (2006, p. 123). This brings in a dimension of structural sin and adds another layer to a principle that has served us well for a number of years.

When we are reflecting it can be useful to go beyond our narrow setting and look to see if there are wider implications that may need action on our part. Thompson talks about oppression at the personal, cultural and structural levels and when we are engaging with culture it can be helpful for us to look beyond the purely personal application (1998, pp. 12–19).

Conclusion

Paul often finds himself seeing an advert or other form of media and thinking, 'I want the Church to be like that.' Cultural texts and not just Jesus or the Bible can be reference points for reflection. We do of course need to use discernment criteria to ensure that we are faithful to our faith as well as taking culture seriously. Reflective practice and theological reflection give us credible

> **?** *What media do you find yourself drawn to or ignore as sources for your reflection?*

115

ways of processing and engaging with our culture. They offer to us processes to take seriously and to listen to both our faith and our world. Both are rich in stimulating concepts and can be used to critique each other and produce reflections and outcomes that sharpen our ministry and mission.

7

Reflecting without words

The true work of art is but a shadow of the divine perfection.
(Michelangelo)

It's on the strength of observation and reflection that one finds a
way. So we must dig and delve unceasingly.   *(Claude Monet)*

Reflecting without words is the tool that we usually get the strongest
reaction to as many of us carry negative perceptions of our ability
to be creative or artistic. Some may turn to this chapter first and
others skip past it. Both of us would at one time have avoided anything arty. Sally was so grateful that at school she could drop all
practical subjects before external exams had to be taken. However,
now artwork is one of the most valued tools in her box. She sometimes needs to explore how she is feeling about an issue because
something is bubbling under the surface but it is hard to get whatever it is to emerge. At these times she uses oil pastels and colour
to reflect. For example, prior to major surgery she explored how
she felt and the potential positive and liberating consequences were
expressed in greens and yellows but there was a small dark patch
which reflected the scary stories she read when researching her condition online and the bit in the consent form which said she might
die from this procedure! The activity helped her to be real about her
fears but see them in proportion to the benefits.

Jeremiah 18 uses the image of God as a potter and this was the
starting point for an exercise Gina led with a group. There were all
sorts of coloured balls of Plasticine and each person was asked to
choose one and create a 'pot' which represented him or her. This led
to a reflection on diversity and uniqueness and an encouragement
to appreciate the way that God had created each person there. It gave
a visual illustration to an issue that had been causing problems

117

within the group and gave an opportunity to talk about the need to treat each other with respect and listen.

Why reflect without words?

In this chapter we explore ways in which we reflect that are not predominantly word-based. One theory of learning styles suggests that some of us learn best visually (see <www.vark-learn.com> for a questionnaire to explore this) so some of the tools described here may be particularly useful. One of the reasons for wanting to explore reflection without words is because it is a way of getting to our feelings rather than reflection remaining a head-based activity. Although ideally feelings should usually be explored as part of being reflective, sometimes this happens more readily when reflecting without words. When we look around our lecture room or training session we sometimes notice people doodling. MacBeth suggests that some people can 'listen and concentrate best when we are seemingly distracted by other activity – in other words, when we are allowed to play'. She goes on to comment that when we are playful we are often at our most honest as we drop our external persona (2007, p. 39). Although not all reflecting without words is necessarily playful, some is and can be a helpful medium for some to access parts of themselves that tend to get buried.

In reflecting without words we will be engaging our imaginations. Our imagination can be a resource to us or an adversary and, as Allen posits, imagination reveals our deepest self, our soul (1995, p. 3). She suggests that making art is a way of exploring our imagination and of exploring more options (1995, p. 4). Cameron values the insight we gain from creative activity; she argues that often it is the ability to read the signs that may be a change for us and can lead to change (1996, p. 118). She wisely suggests that 'Without deliberately cultivated compassion for ourselves, spiritual and creative growth becomes a forced march through the hostile territory of our own judgements' (1996, p. 118).

Inherent in much of the material we have read is the notion of using art therapeutically. Malchiodi notes that 'Throughout history, visual art has been used to make sense of crisis, pain and psychic upheaval' (1998, p. 133). Dalley describes how art can be seen as symbolic speech, as communicating non-verbally through symbols, and that 'symbolizing feelings and experiences in images can be a more powerful means of expression and communication than verbal description, and at the same time, is able to render these feelings and experiences less threatening' (1984, p. xiii). Thus this chapter comes with a warning too: using art may stir up powerful feelings. Any time we engage with making art and reflecting, or ask others to engage in this way, we need to be aware of the potential consequences. This means that we should not use it with a group unless we are sure that we have the skills (or that others who are there do) to help people process some of the deep emotions that may arise. There is a potential risk in many activities but as responsible ministers we do need to assess the potential dangers of activities like this and warn participants of what may emerge and have a plan in place to deal with anything that needs processing beyond the session.

Reflecting without words means that we need to develop our capacity to see, to look, to observe. Hieb counsels us: 'Do not worry about gazing. Authentic seeing is restful, energizing, transforming and completely natural. Seeing will slow you down. Seeing will center you. Seeing will intensify your experiences of the ordinary. Seeing is a creative act' (2005, p. 23).

? *What is your response to reflecting without words? Is this a 'go to' or 'run away' place?*

Visual theology

We first encountered this term when reading Penny Brook's thesis on religion, art and the Australian landscape and really liked what she had to say about how art is theology too. We had used images, sculptures, photographs, etc. for theological reflection but this went further. She writes:

> Visual texts are vital hermeneutical tools in themselves in that they have the capacity to critique and reveal deeper understanding and knowledge of the human condition and the questions that originate within it. Within religious faith, visual images as hermeneutical tools offer the possibility for new understanding and knowledge that enables a better understanding of its past as grounding for more authentic theologising and religious practice within the present human context. (Brook, 2006, p. 345)

119

As part of her thesis Penny Brook had developed some works of art that were designed to be used in worship and stated that:

> The artworks are also meant to function as pedagogical, dialogical and hermeneutical tools. This means that they can be utilised to teach, discuss, debate, critique, deconstruct and reconstruct traditional theological and cultural notions and assumptions in the search for a deeper understanding of the Christian story and therefore of human life.
>
> (Brook, 2006, p. 285)

She also makes the point that historically works of art were often made for a specific site. While this is obvious for something like the ceiling of the Sistine Chapel and some stained-glass windows, we have rarely reflected on the context of the development of works of art in the way that we automatically would do when considering a written text.

We live in Birmingham, where the cathedral is famous for its stained-glass windows designed by Edward Burne-Jones, which tend to evoke strong emotions either way. They are clearly products of their time, pre-Raphaelite images which portray characters in a culturally specific way. When Sally sees them she is taken in her mind to our picture of Holman Hunt's *Light of the World* which we have because it was her grandma's. The images are able to access things in her subconscious that words alone rarely do.

Creative processes

The phrase 'inner images meet paint and paper and inner music becomes the sound of a symphony orchestra' (Darley and Heath, 2008, p. 17) is one way of looking at the creative process. It can be helpful to identify our own images and metaphors that describe what being creative means to us. When reflecting without words there may be stages that we go through which can be helpful to understand (adapted from Malchiodi, 1998, pp. 66–8):

- *Preparation* is vital. It involves getting the materials you need together and preparing yourself for what you want to reflect on and making sure you have articulated the intention you have in your reflection.
- *Incubation* is the stage where you explore the mental image of what it is you are trying to create and see it begin to take shape. As you

begin to create, new elements and ideas may well emerge to be integrated into your art work, which will be most effective if you let
your intuition, improvization and sense of play flourish.

- *Illumination* is the time when you have a breakthrough or 'aha'
moment and you feel a sense of satisfaction with what you have
created.
- *Verification/revision* is the last stage where you may add final
touches to your creation and ensure that it is in the form that you
want.

Signs and symbols

When reflecting using art, signs or symbols may be an integral part
of anything that emerges. In Jungian psychology a sign is a short-
hand way of communicating something that is already known, for
example, a loaf of bread indicating a baker's shop. Symbols are more
dynamic and may emerge from the unconscious. Symbols may hold
more than one meaning and can be interpreted in a variety of ways.
Thus the symbol of a fish in an advertisement may mean that it is a
Christian business or related to surfing, the sea, fishing, etc. If symbols appear in our art or reflection they can help us in exploring and
possibly resolving the issue because a symbol is outside of ourselves
and we may find it easier to engage with it there (Darley and Heath,
2008, pp. 18–19). Thus when we create art we need to be aware that
'all artwork does have a symbolic quality, because it is pregnant with
connection. Pieces relate deeply and dynamically to the artist who
gave birth to them' (Darley and Heath, 2008, p. 21). We may well have
developed our own personal sign and symbolic language. As you
become more practised at this kind of reflection you may recognize
themes and/or images that regularly occur in your work and begin
to see their meaning and importance.

Symbolic acts

Sometimes it is an action that we reflect on or that in retrospect
has meaning. As part of a retreat we led on Cuthbert's Island, in a
Eucharist Paul felt prompted to ask to pour out some of the wine in
the place where we had communion to represent something in his
life that he was working through with God. It spoke to him of
sacrifice and pain; and now when we are on Holy Island looking out

at Cuthbert's Island all the memories come flooding back. It is often said we remember what we do more than what we say or see. It may be that we want to do something together as a group to help people reflect. Of all the things that we have taken part in as Christians one of those that most stands out is the human chain we made in Birmingham as part of the 'Make Poverty History' campaign.

In the chapel of the Children's Hospital in Birmingham the team have worked hard to provide opportunities for children and families to express their feelings and prayers. There are prayer trees that change with the seasons to which people can add a leaf with a prayer or name written on. As you may imagine, Paul does many baptisms in his work at the Children's Hospital. These are more often than not at the end of life or for very ill children. When he started he became aware very quickly of the lack of ability of most of the families who asked for a baptism to express how they felt or join with understanding in any liturgy.

He first introduced the idea of using small gold hearts when a young person was dying and the large wider family, including many children, had gathered around the bedside. As about 30 members of the family gathered in a small room for a blessing of the dying young person, he offered the children an opportunity to place a small gold heart around the body of their brother, cousin, friend. What transpired was most interesting; not only did the children do this but the adults eagerly participated.

Paul has gone on to develop this and now offers a silk forget-me-not (flower) to take away as an indicator that this person will never be forgotten. If Paul conducts a funeral service or family members come back to the hospital they frequently ask for more hearts or forget-me-nots as often other family members want to share the experience and to have something that will prompt a remembrance of the loved one.

Music

Music offers opportunities to reflect without words. It can evoke feelings and memories and may change our mood. Often we choose music that resonates with how we are feeling but we should perhaps choose music to challenge our feelings. Sally remembers while at school listening to *Danse Macabre* by Saint-Saëns and being struck by the strangeness of the chords. The music evoked a midnight-in-the-graveyard-type feeling; perhaps this is an example of a classical emo (a youth subculture) piece. The theme music from Tchaikovsky's *Swan Lake* is another haunting piece of music which can make one feel almost melancholic. Listening to Fleetwood Mac's *Albatross* takes us back to the sea, which brings a different set of feelings. We all have our own examples and hearing others' choices can sometimes be surprisingly revealing.

Tools and exercises for reflecting without words

There are things here we can do in five minutes as an icebreaker at the beginning of a session or some things that can become part of our lives as a regular reflection tool. Sometimes it can be helpful to have questions or topics in mind to respond to. We may have a specific issue we want to focus on but these are ones that we use regularly:

- how do I feel today?
- me as a minister or youth worker or spouse or colleague – or any other role that is significant to you . . .
- my relationship with God or spiritual journey
- places or people that are important
- a specific event in the past, present or future, for example, significant birthday, someone leaving, a bereavement
- the past, present or future in general
- an emotion that you want to understand better.

You could also reflect on a particular Bible passage such as those listed on pages 76–8.

Using colour to reflect

Most of us have clear ideas on colour; we know what we like and don't like, what our 'favourite' colour is and what our first impulse is when choosing something for our house. Hieb suggests that 'Many of the attributes of colour speak to us at the level of our intuition. Colour has great emotional content and usually a long intimate history for individuals' (2005, p. 75). Cameron suggests that there is a scientific basis to our different responses to colour:

> Colour, like sound is made of vibration . . . Red, yellow, blue, green, orange, purple – each vibrates at certain signature frequency. Each

sends out a certain length of wave . . . Another, useful way to think of colour is as visible sound. When we work with colours, we are in effect building visual chords or symphonies.   (Cameron, 1996, p. 123)

Hieb uses the term 'colour vocabulary' (2005, p. 107) to describe the fact that most of us attach significance to colours and observes that we can benefit from exploring this. Malchiodi suggests that we all have a 'personal visual language for expressing our emotional selves' (1998, p. 155) and that some people find colour useful in this process. She goes on to say that 'Although colour may express our thoughts, perceptions, and physical sensations, we most often associate it with emotions' (1998, p. 155).

Malchiodi offers a range of meanings for different colours as a basis to begin reflection (see Table 7.1) but does acknowledge that these meanings can appear contradictory and that our understandings of colour may be culturally determined and are also often unique to us (2005, p. 157).

Table 7.1 Common colour associations (Malchiodi, 1998, p. 157)

Colour	Common associations
Red	Birth, blood, fire, emotion, warmth, love, passion, wounds, anger, heat, life
Orange	Fire, harvest, warmth, energy, misfortune, alienation, assertiveness, power
Yellow	Sun, light, warmth, wisdom, intuition, hope, expectation, energy, riches, masculinity
Green	Earth, fertility, vegetation, nature, growth, cycles of renewal, envy, over-protectiveness, creativity
Blue	Sky, water, sea, heaven, spirituality, relaxation, cleansing, nourishing, calm, loyalty
Purple/Violet	Royalty, spirituality, wealth, authority, death, resurrection, imagination, attention, excitement, paranoia, persecution
Black	Darkness, emptiness, mystery, beginning, womb, unconsciousness, death, depression, loss
Brown	Fertility, soil, sorrow, roots, excrement, dirt, worthlessness, new beginnings
White	Light, virginity, purity, moon, spirituality, creation, timelessness, dreamlike, generativity, resurrection, clarity, loss, synthesis, enlightenment

She offers the following list of questions as aids to help us to reflect on our use of colour:

- How do you use colour in your images to express emotion?
- Do certain colours have specific meanings for you?
- Are there areas of heavy uses of colour? Light uses of colour?
- Do you like to use particular combinations such as black and white; earthy, golden colours; pastels; deep, dark tones; colours found in nature? (Malchiodi, 1998, p. 158)

Hieb talks about using colour as a form of journalling; she makes suggestions as to how to respond to questions such as those listed above:

- Close or focus your eyes and move to a deeper awareness of the topic being considered.
- Visualize the colours/lines/shapes that are your response to the question.
- Go with your 'feel' for colours.
- Be in a receptive attitude.
- Look at yourself as being in dialogue with the colours.
- But try not to think too much – go with your instincts.
- Remember there is no right or wrong way to do the exercise.
- There is no specified end product.
- Usually this will take between 5 and 20 minutes.
- When you have finished reflect on what you have noticed and consider recording it (Hieb, 2005, 29–31).

Sally asked students to respond to the question: 'How do you feel at the end of your first term on the course?' using just colour. As with any activity there were mixed responses but in our experience that often relates to the predominant learning style of the student and how that correlates with the activity. At the positive end one student wrote:

> I found this a very useful activity, it enabled me to express things that I would have found difficult to do so in words, either through speech or in writing. My picture shows that my feelings at the time were unclear, and mixed, which is why it is a mixture of many colours.

Another wrote 'I found this way of expressing myself really helpful' and she saw her image as very positive with colours representing inner calmness and contentment and being excited, energetic and happy. Perhaps the most negative response was one that said, 'I did not find this exercise particularly helpful, and felt that it limited my ability to express myself.'

We always need to be prepared to get such a range of responses in using reflective activities and it is often beneficial to have done them first ourselves before getting other people to do them. Using just colour to reflect can be done individually or in a group and can be part of a regular reflection process in either situation. We can illustrate our journey in colour in the same way that many of us use words.

Collage

'When words fail me, I turn to pictures. Most specifically, I turn to collage' (Cameron, 1996, p. 116). There are many ways to do collage but often having a large pile of varied magazines, large sheets of paper, tissue paper, pens to add lines, words, etc., glue or spray mount (which is useful for repositioning as the idea changes and develops) is enough. Collage helps to answer the question 'What do you see?' As you select images, or colours or shapes, how you feel about what it is you are reflecting on begins to emerge and you can spend time making sense of what you have created. Again, this activity helps in processing, as Cameron suggests: 'because collage bypasses language, you do not need to abstract symbols into words to absorb their meanings' (1996, p. 117).

For example, a retreat facilitator suggested we might want to explore the idea of what we have lost. Going through a magazine and cutting out images and then putting them together helped us to get below the surface and identify things that wouldn't have come to mind without the visual stimuli. There was a picture of Beadnell, which is where we went for our tenth wedding anniversary, and it reinforced our commitment to celebration as a spiritual discipline which sometimes gets lost in the busy nature of everyday life.

Collages can be used corporately too; we can express what we think together through creating a collage. This can be helpful in areas such as vision-building (see Nash *et al.*, 2008). Collage can be useful for people who find drawing or painting difficult and can be good as an activity for those who do not have a lot of experience in reflecting with art as it is easy to amend and change as you go along, and looking at magazines can help as a trigger to ideas.

Pictures

All sorts of pictures can be used for reflection. We may have our favourites or spend time wandering round galleries looking at what resonates with us. If you walk around our house you will see a range of pictures that have meaning for us and that when we see them help us in reflection. Many are golf pictures, which remind Paul of where he has played or watched golf, but others are more symbolic. This is being written in our lounge where we have a picture of the Palace Pier in Brighton, which says fun to us. We visited it in the mad week of preparation for our wedding. It is in a place where neither of us nor our parents lived and our visit was a time to reconnect to the child in us. There is also a picture of the plant honesty in fine detail, which reminds us of the discipline of noticing, really looking and taking in what is around us.

There are many different resources available that offer different images of Christ, and these can be used in a myriad of ways to help people reflect. The last time Sally was in a group and was asked to do this she picked out a child-like drawing as that resonated with what she was feeling at that time. It was at the end of a long and busy academic year so the idea of being a child with Jesus was very attractive. Hodgson asserts that 'Images of Christ are visual iconic representations of the incarnation endowed with colour, shape, contour and movement and embedded in a story, the gospel story of Jesus' (2006, p. 9) but goes on to note that some feel that such images are in violation of the second commandment. When using pictures or other images we need to be aware of any theological or cultural issues there may be and perhaps give some time to developing and articulating a rationale for their use. She suggests that pictures of Christ are just a different way of doing theology and offers a range of ways of working with pictures.

We both enjoy the prayer chapel at Buckfast Abbey. At the end of the chapel is a stained-glass window about the size of the side of an average semi-detached house. Each time we are there something different emerges. Sally thinks of it as seeing her big Jesus; it puts us into perspective and sometimes all we do is just sit and be with Jesus. It is one of our sacred places, a thin place for us where we regularly hear God. Last time we were there what most struck Sally was that Jesus had big eyes and a small mouth and this was a reminder to take more time in seeing before speaking.

Reflecting on pictures is an accessible way of introducing the idea of reflecting without words. Some people collect postcards and other pictures (cinemas often have lots of free ones) or we can ask people to bring one or more of their favourite pictures to share with others.

Images and icons

Our prayer room is full of images and icons that help us reflect and make connections. Both pictures and objects can be used. For example, with a group of youth workers we used a statue of an African woman carrying a sheep around her neck. The shepherd metaphor came quickly to mind but, because it is only upon close inspection that the figure is seen to be a woman, the ideas of female imagery for God were slower to come forth. Issues of Jesus not being white were also raised. Concepts that are difficult for some to begin to deal with because of their own backgrounds or church traditions were easier to engage with through an image.

We also have Rublev's icon of the Trinity, which is an icon in the Orthodox tradition of a sacred painting which can both facilitate worship and teach us. Paul meets with a blind friend regularly and usually when they pray together Paul will give him something to hold to help connect with God; it may be, for example, a Trinitarian image, a cross with symbols on it, a chalice or a stone.

For further reflection
Use the following to trigger your own reflection:

- pruning a rose bush
- a buzzard tearing apart a rabbit
- driving out of mist into clear blue sky and sunshine.

Lines-and-shapes exercises

Think about what it is you want to reflect on – for example, your current state of mind, such as happiness or discontentment – then draw a line on a piece of paper trying to capture the mood. If you have a variety of media to work with and draw on this can help capture your mood. You can do the same with shape also, creating a picture by repeatedly using the same shape (adapted from Barber, 2002, pp. 20–3).

Time-capsule collage

This exercise can be done to reflect on periods of our life, how we feel about a specific situation, looking at the future, exploring a relationship, etc. (technique adapted from Cameron, 1996, p. 119). Take a pile of magazines, newspapers, photographs, catalogues: anything that is in your paper recycling box. Choose around 20 images that resonate with what it is you are exploring through your collage. You don't have to know why the image speaks to you; just recognize that it does at this stage. Then taking 20 minutes or so, lay the images out and add anything you want to with pens or paint, etc. You may want to put the collage somewhere you see it regularly so you can reflect on the meanings that emerge from the process and product.

The window

A picture of a four-paned window can be used in a number of ways. Either draw one or print one out that you have found or created on a computer. We can then draw in each square, in the first our past, in the second the present and in the other two possible futures, what we hope for and fear. This can also be used with a group to look at the story of an organization or as part of a vision-building process. In essence, it could be used for any reflection where we want to look at four elements (adapted from Sunderland and Engleheart, 1993, pp. 22–3).

Mandalas

Mandalas have been used for centuries for spiritual enlightenment across a range of religious traditions. Some of the earliest Christian ones are those of the mystic Hildegard of Bingen from the eleventh century. A mandala is an image which is created within a circle, often with a range of colours. The circle can be any size, although some think that a diameter of 250 mm (10 in.) is good as it is the size of a human head, and others think a circle within a square is good as Jung suggested that this was a representation of the self (Malchiodi, 1998, p. 127). Oil pastels work well for this but choose any media. Sometimes mixed media is effective as texture as well as colour can be significant.

- Draw a circle on a suitably sized piece of paper.
- The circle can be filled in however we like, using anything we like. It doesn't matter where we start, whether it is geometric or not,

or whether we go outside of the circle. There is no right or wrong way to draw it but for future reference it can be useful to make it clear which way up it goes. Putting a place and a date may help evoke the wider memories associated with it.

- Displaying the mandala can help get the most out of our reflection and sometimes we see something we didn't realize first time round.

Sally was on a retreat and decided she would use mandalas as her means of reflection. She worked on four over the few days there. The first explored the theme of the retreat, the second an issue from her past that still caused her concern, the third was prompted by one of the sessions and the final one was a reflection on something God had said. The series of four are now a very visual reminder of what she experienced on the retreat. Darley and Heath suggest drawing a light and dark mandala using different lead pencils and exploring things that we associate with both light and dark and integrating them into one mandala, which helps us to see how different elements can co-exist in our lives (2008, p. 153).

Metaphorical portraits

This involves drawing ourselves as an object – such as a house, animal, food, tree, flower, island, building, plant, landscape, car, bird, game or place – and where appropriate add a context. We may then reflect on what we chose and why. Trigger questions include:

- What object would you like to be?
- What object represents how you feel today?
- What animal, etc. would you most or least like to be?
- If you were a seed what point of growth would you be at? (adapted from Liebmann, 2004, pp. 228–9).

Life path

Many of us will have used life graphs where we mark the ups and downs of our lives over the years. Another possibility is to imagine our life as a journey and draw or model this journey in clay using symbols as they resonate with us. This may mean a journey on a road, a landscape, a sea voyage, a trip to the moon – whatever helps us to explore and explain our life. This can be done in pairs where we explain our journey to each other and talk about how we felt at different stages on the journey. It is also possible, where appropriate, to ask the other person how they respond to our journey (adapted from Sunderland and Engleheart, 1993, pp. 10–11). Other adaptations include focusing on one section of our life; working on one facet, such as vocation or family; having sections for past, present and future; and drawing a maze, spiral, map or cartoon strip (Liebmann, 2004, p. 230).

Trunks and dustbins

We often have two sorts of difficult experiences and emotions. Some we want to discard and hopefully never see again; and some we don't feel able to deal with now, or we are aware of but not to the extent that we feel we want to deal with them. The first set of emotions needs to go in the dustbin and the second in a trunk so that we can access them when we are ready or when we need to. Draw a picture of both and representations of what needs to go in them (adapted from Liebmann, 2004, p. 236).

Letting go with clay

In this exercise we think about something we would like to let go of and then fashion it in clay; it may be something either concrete or abstract. We can then decide if we would like to destroy what we have created, or throw it away, or make some other symbolic act that helps us to let go of something, such as giving it to someone else, burying it, pouring water over it to symbolize cleansing (adapted from Darley and Heath, 2008, p. 151).

Photographs

Taking photos is another way in which reflection without words can be expressed. With the capacity today to download pictures onto our computers rather than pay to have them printed out there are endless opportunities for capturing moments for future reflection.

Conclusion

We regularly introduce activities where people can reflect without words, such as those mentioned above, into quiet days, teaching sessions and church-based groups. However, in contexts where people are not familiar with such activities we will usually have them as options with other more familiar word-based activities such as reading a Bible passage and answering some questions or writing a prayer or just sitting and reflecting quietly. We would then have a period of feedback at the end of an exercise. Often people are encouraged into trying such activities by the experience of others who share in such a way that newcomers want to have a go next time.

Another approach is for us to tell a story or to have asked someone else to be willing to share at the beginning of the day or session to help people understand that what is important is the process and what you learn from doing something rather than the 'quality' of the product. We also always set ground rules which make it clear that people can choose whether or not they share and that they will never be put on the spot. If you want to consider introducing such activities then it is worth collecting a range of materials including:

- paper in different sizes and colours including on a roll
- oil pastels, pencils, charcoal, felt tips and marker pens
- paints – children's squeezy bottle-type paints work well – paint brushes, palettes, jars for water
- plastic cloths or decorating sheets to protect furniture or the carpet
- glue and spray mount
- collage materials, which can be anything, for example, pulses, small buttons, sequins, old magazines, wool or tissue paper.

Bargain bookshops often have such materials on sale quite cheaply. For a group completely new to such activities we would start with simple exercises like reflecting on pictures or music, and then perhaps do a simple colour exercise where participants respond to a less personal topic such as 'the state of our nation' or 'our community' before asking people to engage with something that requires personal disclosure at any level.

> **?** *How does your reflection give you opportunity to engage with and process your feelings? Are there additional tools you need to add?*

Reflecting without words often enables us to access the parts of us that other forms of reflection don't reach. It can help us connect at an emotional level and explore what is going on in our lives at greater depth. This is perhaps why some of the ways of reflecting outlined here evoke a strong reaction. Chapter 6 on observing culture and the awareness nature walks from Chapter 8 obviously connect with the ideas in this chapter as very accessible ways of not using words for reflection.

8

Reflecting with nature

Understand the creation, if you wish to know the Creator.
(Columbanus)

I look up at your macro-skies, dark and enormous, your hand-made sky-jewelry, moon and stars mounted in their settings . . .
GOD, brilliant Lord, your name echoes around the world.
(Psalm 8, The Message)

Nature is not only all that is visible to the eye. It also includes the inner pictures of the soul. *(Edvard Munch)*

We are on a lifelong quest to understand more of God, ourselves and our ministries and one of the things this book is trying to do is to show ways into this. Because in essence nature is God's creation, a revelation, a way of seeing him, reflecting on nature can be particularly fruitful. An extract from Sally's journal in January 2007 reads:

> I cannot really describe the sense of anticipation I felt in arriving at the place I hoped would fulfil a long-held dream [Lapland where I hoped to see the Northern Lights]. It is that funny mix of hope and fear. As an introvert it often feels like I live in my head and sometimes I don't really notice what is going on in the world around me. However, that was not true at night time, in the outdoors, hoping, just hoping for a glimpse. It reminded me of when I was a new Christian and that's how I felt about God and the work of the Holy Spirit in my life. What would happen next? Where would I see God? How might he speak to me? My first experience was looking into the darkness, into the night sky which was pierced by stars – tiny pockets of light that always remind me how vast the universe is, and how big my God is. We did see glimpses of the Northern Lights on the Saturday night and the word that best described those to me was 'dancing', this green phenomenon danced across the sky, shimmering, beautiful, coming and going with seemingly no rhyme or reason.

However, it was the Sunday night where we saw what was one of the best displays of the season. Sunday evening was the highlight of the trip – snowmobiles across the frozen river into the wilderness for a meal cooked in a wooden hut with a barbecue in the middle. We had barely begun our meal when someone came in and announced, 'They're here!' Now I am not renowned for leaving food uneaten but this was something that I had travelled miles for and had longed to see for so many years; perhaps I felt a little of what Simeon experienced when he finally felt he had seen the Messiah. I felt so privileged. Here I was, in the middle of nowhere, and here was this most amazing display of nature's creativity put on for a few of us. I kept scanning the sky for a glimpse of the next flash, the next wave, the next shimmering magical phenomenon that filled me with awe, helped me experience the mysterious, the magical, what seemed to be the miraculous. The only way you could fully appreciate it was to lie down on your back in the snow to look up at the sky and see the aurora borealis in all its glory. I was contemplating God's greatness and majesty through this display of his magical creativity. It will live with me forever. I am challenged by my sense of anticipation, my passion and enthusiasm and sense of awe. I want all of that to be part of my relationship with God regularly, not as a special one-off. I have memories of the feelings and emotions, the excitement. I felt playful and childlike, overwhelmed and caught up with the moment. It took me out of my grown-up world and reminded me of what it was like to be a child where things are special and exciting, not jaded and disappointing.

Examples of reflection on nature

We often write in places with a view out of the window and a glance outside can bring inspiration. Really looking or noticing can bring deeper insight and we can learn something more of God, ourselves, others and our ministry. Henri Nouwen wrote a prayer every day when he was on retreat at a monastery. This is one example of the many that draw on nature:

Dear Lord, the unexpected snow today made me think how careful I have to be in making predictions. Just when I had prepared myself for spring and gentler, sunnier weather, winter seemed to return. Aren't you giving me an important warning? (1981, p. 72)

Sally did something similar for a season, writing each day about what she saw out of the prayer-room window. She noted in her journal that:

> A flock of terns have just flown over, it reminded me of summer days to come, days of warmth and blue. It occurred to me that we are very landlocked here in Birmingham and that the terns are a long way from home, and that is an image we carry with us. We are a long way from home but are trying to create home, a dwelling place wherever we can, but we need to hold on lightly to where we are and be willing to move on for the sake of the kingdom. But the Benedictine rule of stability helps me to see that there is value in staying in one place too.

This is Sally's favourite prayer by Henri Nouwen, which she uses a lot. She has created a picture around it, which hangs in her study:

> Dear Lord, Today I thought of the words of Vincent Van Gogh 'It is true there is an ebb and flow, but the sea remains the sea.' You are the sea. Although I experience many ups and downs in my emotions and often feel great shifts and changes in my inner life, you remain the same. Your sameness is not the sameness of a rock, but the sameness of a faithful lover. Out of your love I came to life; by your love I am sustained, and to your love I am always called back. There are days of sadness and days of joy; there are feelings of guilt and feelings of gratitude; there are moments of failure and moments of success; but all of them are embraced by your unwavering love. My only real temptation is to doubt in your love, to think of myself as beyond the reach of your love, to remove myself from the healing radiance of your love. To do these things is to move into the darkness of despair. O Lord, sea of love and goodness, let me not fear too much the storms and winds of my daily life, and let me know that there is ebb and flow but that the sea remains the sea. (Nouwen, 1981, pp. 143–4)

The sea is what most brings life to Sally, and reflections about the sea most often attract her. For example, Halverson suggests that 'We may never solve all the mysteries of the sea, but we can take those mysteries, along with our basic knowledge, and use them to search out the character of God' (1999, p. 11). Keller also uses the sea to provide a book full of reflections that help us to see God's work in our lives:

> We cry from the depths: 'Who can cover my iniquities? Who can enfold me in righteousness? Who can fill me with the fullness of God?' It is

He and only He who can do this for us. There is no one else. And we must see this. The beach does not cover itself. It is covered by the sea. The shore does not change itself. It is shaped by the tides. The sea edge does not diminish its own size. The ocean does this as it sweeps in upon it. The alterations and rearrangements of the coast are the eternal work of the eternal tides. And in my life as one who lies open, exposed and receptive to the action of The Most High, it is He who will cover and conform me to His own pattern of ultimate perfection.

(1985, pp. 27–8)

Another reflection that has been sustaining is Julian of Norwich's vision of a hazelnut

in the palm of my hand, and it was as round as a ball. I looked thereupon with the eye of my understanding and thought, 'What may this be?' And it was generally answered this, 'It is all that is made.' I marvelled how it might last, for I thought it might suddenly have fallen to nought for littleness. And I was answered in my understanding, 'It lasts and ever shall, for God loves it.' And so all things have their being by the love of God. In this little thing I saw three properties. The first is that God made it; the second that God loves it; the third that God keeps it.

(2003, pp. 8–9)

One of the challenges of reflecting with nature is to see God in the less lovely elements or places where we may not normally look. Rupp offers this challenge

If I only look for God in the good things of my life, I will miss many facets of this loving presence. I need to focus on the unwanted, the uncomfortable, and the unexpected parts of my life . . . We can ask ourselves: Do I look for God's presence in the angry driver yelling obscenities, in the physician who misdiagnosed a critical illness, in the jailed drug dealer, in the uncooperative neighbour who makes life miserable for others, in the child who lies and cheats, in the politician who has opposing views, in the family member who shuns me?

(2001, p. 53)

We have lived in urban areas for most of our married life and have come to really appreciate this perspective. God is in all of creation, not just the pretty bits! Here Seddon is reflecting on a tin can:

On the water I can see a large can, now fairly close to the shore. The can is being swept this way and that, by the incoming tide. As I watch, it is swept way to my right, out of sight. I thought, Lord, how easily we can be like that, adrift, and swept along by the tide and events of life. Lord, we sometimes mistake this being adrift for freedom – it isn't, for without you as our anchor, our rudder and our sails, we are not free, we're lost. Lord, help us to hold firm to our faith in you, to anchor ourselves to you, lest we drift aimlessly, at the mercy of all that life can do to us.   (undated, p. 26)

For further reflection

Use the following to trigger your own reflection:

- How do you grow?
- Different types of soil.
- Nurture, water, sun, fertilizer.
- Picture some seagulls in a field.
- How might we think and act if we found out we were the only human being-like creatures in the universe?
- Some house plants grow towards the sun and shed leaves so others can grow.

Using our senses

In reflecting on nature and the environment our senses particularly come into play. Dunn argues that life is experienced through our senses but that we respond differently depending on the context, and some situations are overwhelming and others are calming. She writes, 'Sensation is everywhere. Not only are people sensory beings, the world is a sensory place as well. The world around us makes sounds, provides textures, offers tastes and smells, and contains a myriad things to see' (2008, p. 17). We make decisions daily based on our sensory preferences; for example, Paul doesn't like the texture of smooth silk and the smell of a fried egg makes Sally feel sick. Such sensations impact what we eat, where we go and so on (Dunn, 2008, p. 27).

Understanding a little of how we use our senses and the preferences we have in doing this can enhance our experience of reflecting on nature and other aspects of our environment. Dunn categorizes four ways we respond but also suggests that our response can be context-specific:

- Seekers always want more sensation and often try and create it wherever they can and will change their routine to get it.
- Bystanders don't know what they are missing because they don't notice what others may do; because of their easy-going nature, it can seem to others that they are not paying attention.
- Avoiders choose routine and order and prefer to work to a plan; they don't need much sensory information and enjoy time alone.
- Sensors are very observant and like to keep track of everything. They will have strong opinions about elements of their environment and can find it hard if it is not to their liking (Dunn, 2008, pp. 33–41).

What we find useful about such a theory is that it helps us understand that in groups this is a further dynamic we need to bear in mind. In encouraging reflection on nature and the environment, people come from a range of different starting points. For some it will be a valuable new window on God, the world or themselves and for others it all may seem a little bit of a waste of time as it is not their preferred way of working or is taking them out of their comfort zones.

Seasons

One of the delights of reflecting on nature is that it is ever changing but follows a pattern. You can do the same walk at different times of the year and experience new things each time. Seasons resonate with our lives too and it can be so helpful to realize that, just as other parts of God's creation experience autumn, winter, spring and summer, so sometimes do we.

Realizing that winter can follow the autumn period of fruitfulness and seeding and that it is time for inner, invisible growth, for example, can be reassuring. We love blackberrying in the autumn and have bags in the freezer to keep a supply of apple-and-blackberry crumbles going all through the winter. Eating the crumble takes us back to the experience of picking the blackberries, the purple-stained fingers, the scratches from the brambles and the careful avoidance of all the lower fruit that may have been targeted by dogs! Winter brings Christmas, Sally's birthday, Valentine's day, celebrations amidst the short dark days, the fog, the rain, the cold and those wonderful days where there is frost, sun and an ice-blue sky. Winter is the time we can see things more clearly; the leaves are gone, the hidden lake reappears and the statue of St John that tops our local church is again to be seen from our bedroom window! When it appears that less is happening that can give us the space and clarity to reflect on issues that we were too busy to think about in the hectic pace of summer.

Spring is exciting. It's when new shoots begin to appear, great for those of us who enjoy innovation and change. It's a season of changes; it seems like nearly summer but all of a sudden winter can be back. We remember snow in early May one year. It takes a while to be confident that the frosts are not going to reappear and kill off the delicate plants.

Then there is summer. It is summer as we are writing this. Outside there are flowers, ripening apples and an abundance of different greens; so many varied shades. There is a huge hydrangea and the flowers are cerise, the bishop's colour, a handy reminder to pray for the Church of England! The signs that we saw in spring are now fully visible; the garden is blossoming. It feels like everything is right in the world on warm sunny days and balmy evenings. It's good to remind ourselves that autumn is on the way.

Tools for reflecting with nature

Awareness walk

As well as being good for our physical health, walking is good for our spiritual health. Cameron believes that walking provides 'thought for food. Walking, with its constant flow of new images, gives us new thoughts that nourish us (1996, p. 25). She notes that 'across cultures and continents, walking is an ancient and literal form for pursuing a spiritual path' (1996, p. 26). Although we may not fully agree with the philosophy behind her recommendation we have found it true for us. Walking provides the space to think and reflect or talk and reflect, and all that we see while we are out can provide future or present resources for reflection. We regularly go walking near water. From home we stroll around filled gravel pits at a council-run country park. Each time the place speaks to us of redemption; something that once scarred the landscape is now a place of beauty, a refuge for birds, local and migrating, and a place of leisure for many people from miles around. Just being there reminds us of one of the most significant aspects of our faith.

An awareness walk involves focusing on the area where we are walking. We use each of our five senses to appreciate all that we encounter and use the walk to give us a greater insight into God. Awareness walks are best done as a deliberate exercise but sometimes it can be helpful to be particularly attentive as we go about our everyday journeys. Sometimes we need to start briskly to warm up but soon we need to amble along slowly. Then we need to become aware of the sensations we experience: the sun's warmth, the drizzle, the cold air, wisps of mist, shadows, breeze, the sky, clouds and so on. Then we need to use our five senses to truly immerse ourselves into the environment. This is a framework we use:

- *Look* at patterns, shapes, heights and depths, colours, stillness and movement.
- *Touch* different objects, sharp, rough, smooth, textures.
- *Listen* to far-off sounds, near sounds, your breathing, birds and animals, traffic, people, water, music, trains, buses, PA systems.
- *Smell* the air, things in the earth, things around, food, perfume, fumes.
- *Taste* is completely at your discretion!
- *Focus* on one thing in detail, something that you are drawn to. Become more aware of it, look at it closely. What does it mean to you at this time?

Ask yourself:

- Where is God in what I am experiencing?
- What could God be saying to me through this?
- What can I learn about God?
- What can I learn about myself?

If it is appropriate (and not breaking any conservation regulations) it can be nice to take something back with you to remind you of what God said or, if doing this exercise as part of a group, to share with others.

Urban awareness walk

As people with a long-term commitment to living and working in an urban context we have also been challenged to go on awareness walks in our local community where it is also possible to see God and hear him speak. We ask ourselves questions as we view our every-day world of buildings, transport, people working, shops, sports, etc. One of the ways Paul has found it helpful to see God in the city is to look for the image of God in the faces that we meet during our everyday activities. This was particularly valuable when he was parish-based and walking around the area. It has been suggested that if photos were taken of every face in the whole world and super-imposed on each other then the face that would come out would be the face of Christ. C. S. Lewis suggests that:

> Next to the Blessed Sacrament itself, your neighbour is the holiest object presented to your senses. If he is your Christian neighbour he is holy in almost the same way, for in him also Christ *vere latitat* – the glorifier and the glorified, Glory Himself, is truly hidden.
>
> (1942, p. 9)

Seeing God in creation

If doing this in a group, collect a number of examples of flowers, leaves, stones, shells or feathers, then either offer people different varieties of the same thing or different objects. Ask them to spend some time in silence with their object, answering the question: 'How does this speak to you of God?' You can then feed back in pairs or small groups. You can also encourage creative responses such as prayers, poems and pictures that may help others see the connection too.

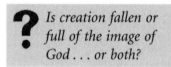

Is creation fallen or full of the image of God . . . or both?

Weather with us

There is a Crowded House song which talks about how we take the weather with us. The weather provides us with an amazing set of metaphors and insights into where we are, our feelings, the stage in our ministry and so on. As a group exercise this can be done with pictures, encouraging people to reflect on the one they feel most drawn to. Leder offers this insight:

> For clouds create a calm mood. Life's sharp shadows are erased. There's no need to don dark glasses to save your eyes from a solar assault.

The nimbus and cumulus protect you. The world is at rest, cuddled down beneath a comforter, flung across the sky. Clouds give us permission to be where we are: a little depressed perhaps, or lazy, or introspective, or just plain quiet as we sip a cup of tea. When in such moods, a bright day can seem accusatory: get up, get going, get cheerful! The sun stares down like a yellow happy face, demanding response in kind. But a cloudy day protects and accepts us. If the sky clouds over, so may we. (2004, p. 35)

Biblical nature parables and illustrations

Meditate upon one of the nature illustrations or parables found in Matthew's Gospel. For example: 6.26–27 – the birds; 6.28–34 – the lilies; 7.17–20 – fruit; 8.23–27 – the storm; 12.11–12 – the sheep; 13.1–23 – the sower; 13.24–30 – the weeds; 13.31–32 – the mustard seed; 13.44 – the treasure; 13.45–46 – the pearl; 13.47–50 – the net; 18.10–14 – the lost sheep; 24.32–33 – the fig tree; 25.31–46 – the sheep and the goats.

Write your own psalm

Using Psalm 1, 8 or 104 as a guide write your own psalm, also using creation imagery.

Four seasons trees

Divide a piece of paper into four squares and in each square draw a (deciduous!) tree which represents the four seasons. Reflect on these questions:

Autumn

- What is changing in your life or ministry?
- What may need to die?
- What do you need to let go of?

Winter

- What areas in your life or ministry are barren?
- Where do you get your nourishment and protection from?
- What do you feel cold about? Is there anything you need to do about this feeling?

Spring

- Where is the new life emerging?
- What are you hopeful about?
- Which seeds don't seem to have taken root?

Summer

- Where do you feel most fruitful?
- What roots you?
- What is coming next that you need to prepare for?

Conclusion

Nature is a wonderful resource for our reflections. It speaks loud and clear if we only listen, look and even touch or smell (perhaps speaking is reserved for the plants!). Images and metaphors spring out at every turn to surprise us both in rural and urban areas. The scope for interpretation is vast and the conclusions immense. The beautiful and ugly both have the potential to speak. There is never a time we cannot reflect on our surroundings and we can be very British and talk about the weather to our heart's content!

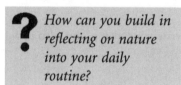

How can you build in reflecting on nature into your daily routine?

9

Reflecting together

No matter who we are or where we come from, we were all born to work together. It's like music – lots of notes make one perfect tune! *(Babette Cole)*

We need a community of inquiry. Such a community cherishes its critics, those inside and those beyond, because it understands that the prophetic voice and word of God are often spoken by those we do not really want to hear. *(Anita Farber-Robertson)*

This book is a consequence of our reflecting together. We each have written different elements but many of the ideas and concepts have been developed for ministry contexts as we spend time together, particularly in the car on long journeys, but also as we have been together with colleagues, students and friends sharing, exploring, chilling and discovering more about ourselves, each other, our faith and our God. This chapter focuses on some of the ways we and others have benefitted from reflecting together. In *Skills for Collaborative Ministry* (Nash *et al.*, 2008) there are chapters on group processes and facilitating skills which we recommend you read to help you get the most out of reflecting together.

? *What encourages you to, or might hinder you from, reflecting with others?*

While in other chapters we have introduced a range of activities that may be used with groups, most often this involves individual reflection within the group context. This chapter focuses on ways a group works together in reflection and corporate responses emerge.

Inclusion, control and affection

When reflecting together it can be useful to have in mind some frameworks that can help us interpret what may be happening. Schutz (1958) identifies inclusion, control and affection as three basic social needs that we all require, though they may be fulfilled in different ways (see <www.businessballs.com> for an accessible summary). Sometimes such a framework can provide us with the inspiration or the missing jigsaw piece in a reflection and it can help us see where we need to move to next. Inclusion refers to degrees of belonging and feelings about being included or excluded. As a group begins, individuals need to count the cost of joining and explore to what extent they can be authentic in this context. Control is about power, influence and authority and a desire to make a difference. It can involve an individual's approaches to structure and hierarchy, and perceptions of being on the top or bottom. Affection is about being close and far emotionally, being liked and loved. If we don't feel a degree of affection we may become alienated. There are two dimensions to this: how we express these needs and how we want them expressed back to us. Part of growing together as a group can involve a willingness to share our needs in some of these areas, as the way we manifest them varies and we do not always interpret people accurately.

> **?** *Can you see inclusion, affection and control at work in any of your groups?*

Ground rules

In any group activity, particularly a regular group, it can be helpful to set ground rules, as boundaries can make people feel safer. When we do this we usually negotiate them with the group, adding anything we feel is important to their suggestions. It can be helpful to have a list of them in a public place to refer to if needed. The sort of areas that usually emerge are around: listening, respect, confidentiality, valuing each other, being open to the views of others, preparation, mutual responsibility for making the group work, honesty, engaging with conflict and time-keeping.

Building activities

We train youth workers and it is always fascinating seeing people who spend lots of time doing activities with people respond to having to do something similar themselves! If we want to reflect well together then there needs to be a commitment to being open and honest with one another and being willing to be vulnerable and share something of who we are.

Paul chairs the meetings of the Grove Youth Series Editorial Group <www.grove.co.uk> and he begins each meeting with a reflection time. The September 2008 meeting started with Paul sharing his theological reflection on the topic of 'short selling' (this is the practice of selling borrowed shares in the hope of buying them later at a lower price and thus making a profit). We were all then encouraged to share our perspective on it too. Sally learnt things in that meeting about people she thought she already knew quite well. She doesn't know if it was anything to do with the way we began but it was a particularly helpful and creative meeting.

There are lots of books that have icebreakers and putting the term into Google got over 700,000 hits! The skill is in the careful selection and suitability of the activity. We would generally suggest that you never do anything with a group that makes you feel uncomfortable and that with a new group people have the capacity to opt in at a level that feels right for them.

One example is a game where you all write on separate slips of paper three things about yourself that you think others won't know. You collect the slips in, pull one out at random and then people guess who it is about. You can choose your level of disclosure by what you write. Variations on the bingo game with a grid where you collect signatures for different categories, e.g. green eyes, speaks French, can work as individuals choose what they own up to.

Another way into some meaningful activities is using Pip Wilson's blob figures <www.pipwilson.com>. There are trees, scenes, emotions, all sorts of contexts available and it is the sort of activity you can enter into at a range of levels in response to such a question as, 'Which blob figure do you identify with?' Sharing reflections on a picture, object, etc. is another possibility, as is sharing something of value – a favourite book, film scene, song, etc. – or answering a question such as, 'What's your favourite sacred place?' or, 'Which metaphor for place currently summarizes where you are at?'

We have also used an adapted version of Carter's 4 P exercise (1997, p. 114). Divide a sheet of paper into four and complete each quarter with:

- a person who has been influential on your spiritual journey
- a place that is sacred to you
- a period where your spiritual journey took a new direction
- a passion that you have.

Communities of practice

The concept of 'communities of practice' is often associated with Wenger (1998) who defines them as 'groups of people who share a concern or passion for something they do and learn how to do it better as they interact regularly' <www.ewenger.com>. Communities of practice have three essential elements: the domain, the community and the practice. Thus, for example, our domain would be youth ministry, our community the Centre for Youth Ministry, and our practice would be the teaching of youth ministry. Domain, community and practice exist when people learn together. Not all groups can be categorized as such and often there needs to be an intentionality in the learning for a community of practice to function properly. Sometimes when you get together with others in similar roles it seems more of a case of 'Look how good I am!' rather than 'What can we learn from each other?' A regular 'community of practice' meeting may be a little easier to explain to a manager than having coffee with some mates, but those who do such things regularly testify to the benefits and support it brings.

Frontier Youth Trust <www.fyt.org> were involved in some research into a series of meetings called 'Coffee Shop Theology'. These meetings reflected on a series of issues such as, 'How do we reflect?', 'How do we stay contextual?' and 'What about sustaining ourselves?' Some groups have carried on meeting. Feedback showed how much the event was appreciated: 'Just getting together with other practitioners and like-minded people was really encouraging. It was great to know that there are others out there who are wrestling with the same stuff and asking the same questions!'

Table 9.1 Stages of group development (Sofield *et al.*, 1998, p. 23)

Stage	Expressed feeling or behaviour	Predominant need	Function of a leader	Tasks of a leader
1 Orientation	Anxiety, fear or insecurity	Safety and security	Create a climate where people feel safe and secure	Clarify expectations
2 In/out	Fight, flight or neurotic behaviour	Belonging	Help those alienated to experience a sense of belonging	Encourage those who feel alienated to discuss their perceptions
3 Up/down	Competitiveness	Esteem	Initiate a process that fosters personal value esteem	Utilize a gift discernment process
4 Conflict	Avoidance or denial	Safety and esteem	Encourage the community to deal with conflict	Model a willingness to deal with conflict
5 Cohesion	Peace and trust, tendency to nest	Belonging	Call the group to its mission	Challenge the community to focus beyond itself
6 Faith-sharing	Ambivalence	Safety and esteem	Invite the community to engage in faith-sharing	Model faith-sharing
7 Near/far	Struggle to find a comfort level	Love or affinity	Aid the community to clarify expectations of intimacy	Invite members to discussion expectations of intimacy
8 Termination	Sadness and anger	Safety	Help the community process the experience of loss	Assist the community with the process of grieving

> ? *Is there a group that is or could be a community of practice for you?*

Some people have these networks already, whether a clergy cell or a youth worker support group, but if you don't or it isn't working for you why not try developing a community of practice around your specialism? As we are writing this Paul is involved in establishing a network of specialist paediatric hospital chaplains which hopefully will evolve into a community of practice with a ready source of colleagues who understand some of the issues and contexts.

Tools and exercises for reflecting together

Evaluating our life together

There are different ways we can evaluate our life together. These questions were developed by Widdicombe (2001, p. 183) for use by small religious communities. However, they may be useful for a ministry team or other close-knit group. Possible questions include:

- What energizes us? What drains us?
- What pulls us apart? What draws us together?
- What have we struggled with?
- How have we used or not used our failures?
- What have we found problematic, unhelpful, a hindrance, hard to tackle or dysfunctional?
- What helps us to persevere when the going gets tough?
- What doubts or hesitations do we have?
- What do we feel uneasy about?
- What do we feel confident about?
- What are we doing well? Not doing so well? What gaps are there?
- What are our strengths and weaknesses?
- What do we find life-giving, individually and as a community?
- What helps and hinders us from functioning well together?
- What builds up our morale?

Another way to evaluate our life together is to measure it against stages of development. One we particularly like has been developed by Sofield *et al.* (see Table 9.1). Questions to ask include:

- Which stage are we at?
- What are the key questions and issues we need to confront at this stage?
- What do we need to address to continue to grow?
- What are the blockages or obstacles that make it hard to grow?

What sort of fish?

An exercise Sally has used in a range of contexts but largely with student groups is the fish in the sea, aquarium or pond. It is a visual way of seeing how individuals see themselves in relation to the group. You draw a fishbowl or sea scene on a large sheet of paper – we usually add in hooks, rocks, weed, etc. Each individual then has a small piece of paper to draw themselves as a fish in relation to how they see themselves in the group. Individuals then cut out their fish and one by one come and stick their fish on to the larger sheet, locating themselves in the picture and explaining (to the extent that they want to) why they drew themselves as they did and why they are locating themselves where they did. If you keep the picture you can also use it to revisit a group after a period of time and see movements in group dynamics, changes in self-perception and so on. Fish vary enormously in size and colour, from tiny dark fish hiding among the weeds to large brightly striped fish in the middle of everything that is happening. It helps people to reflect on where they are in the group and gives insights to others that might not be accessible in other ways.

Shades of grey

Twenty-five years ago Paul used a decision game as part of the selection process for volunteers with Youth for Christ. Two opposing positions would be given and one side of the room would be labelled with one position and the other side of the room would be labelled with the other position; for example, 'Did you choose God or did God choose you?' or, 'Do you prefer *X Factor* or *Strictly Come Dancing*?' or, 'Is it ever right to positively discriminate?' Candidates would then have to go and stand at either side of the room or place themselves somewhere between the two extremes. Asking people to justify their position can then help to understand choices made and where they are coming from. Some will enjoy the opportunity to be more active and engage more kinaesthetically. We have since seen many variations of this, as an icebreaker or research tool, for example.

Question and answer

As part of our ministry module we have a panel where students ask staff and each other anything they like related to the current module. There is always the option to put a question on paper so it can be anonymous. We have seen this done with young people where a question is drawn out of a box that anyone can access and the whole group corporately tries to answer it. The first question we were asked this year was, 'What would you say now to your younger self starting out in ministry?' This question drew out insights that had not been covered in other parts of the teaching.

The gallery

An exercise we do with various groups is to encourage them to put together displays which draw together responses to a range of questions. This is done through art, PowerPoint, large posters, displays, installations, music and so on. We give them time to prepare, to look round individually; then by turn everyone introduces their pieces and answers questions. This exercise can be done in a day or over a couple of evenings and provides a deep understanding of perceptions on a particular topic. For example, we would have a holistic personal vision for ministry as our overarching task and then encourage reflection on some of the activities listed below (which can be adapted for other contexts). In our case, individuals do each of these activities but it could be that you would get people to work individually or in small groups to do one of them:

- List those activities that will facilitate your leading a holistic lifestyle and flourishing in ministry.
- List the principles and values that you work to.
- Compile a list of secular songs that describe how or how not to do ministry and Christian songs that reflect how you want to live and minister.
- What theological perspectives, statements and biblical metaphors best describe your ministry?
- What theoretical models have shaped and influenced your ministry?

- What image holds together your formation?
- Write a creed, an 'I have a dream . . .' (for more on this, see pp. 92–3), a charter, ten commandments, all I know about ministry I learnt from . . . or a covenant.
- What films, advertisements, stories or other media have influenced how you understand ministry and what you want for those you work with?
- Who are your heroes and role models?
- Write a prayer, poem, song, or draw a picture, etc. that reflects an element of your ministry.
- What five to ten Scriptures shape the way you think about and do ministry?
- What metaphors of ministry resonate with you?
- What are the essential tasks of ministry for you?
- What is your praxis of ministry?
- How would you describe your leadership style?
- What temptations may disqualify you from ministry?
- What has happened that holds you back in ministry?
- What are some significant paradigm shifts in ministry?
- What lies about yourself or ministry have you listened to?
- Where do you find your worth, identity, purpose, significance? Are there places you are tempted to find these where you should not?

What emerges from questions such as these is inspirational. In response to the question, 'What image holds together your formation?' Amy Kirby wrote:

> These are photos of two of the many things that bring me back to perspective – that my God made this, the ocean and galaxies. This holds together my formation because it reminds me that he is God, there's nothing bigger or better than him, and it's in him I need to be based and rely.

Laura Pratt listed the principles and values that she works to:

- all young people are made in the image of God and the image of a creative Creator
- holistic salvation and redemption-of-all salvation
- hope
- discipleship/development
- freedom of thought

- valuing individuality and diversity
- valuing process as well as product
- practical love.

Another identified three paradigm shifts:

- God has faith in me – addressing feelings of doubt, reflecting on Peter walking on the water.
- God loves me for who I am not what I do – tempted to do lots to feel worthy.
- ministry is not about one person walking ahead – community.

Reading the signs of the times

Jesus exhorts us in Matthew 16.2–3 to read the signs of the times. It feels funny to write this at what we hope is the height of the credit crunch! We are not always very good at reading the signs of the times and have never bought or sold a house at 'the right time' although each time we have both been sure that it was God who drew us to the place. We had just got engaged and Paul was away and Sally was out house-hunting on her own. She had seen a house she really liked and Paul had a word from God that confirmed it was the house for us without knowing what she had seen. When we couldn't sell it after God called us on, we were still convinced that we had heard right and we ended up renting the house out to missionaries. In reading the signs of the times we need to use both our natural wisdom and the discernment of the Holy Spirit and spending time doing this together will hopefully mean a fuller and more rounded picture.

This exercise is adapted from an idea in Widdicombe (2001, pp. 231–2). If you are going to do something like this it is worth giving the group notice so they can begin to reflect and gather data and ideas. In a group it is likely that people access their news and information in different ways and it may be good to ask people to focus on a particular medium. Set a question such as, 'What strikes us as we look around us today?' or, 'What are the needs and key issues for today?' You may choose to do this at a local, national or international level or anywhere in between! At the beginning of the meeting read Luke 12.54–56 a couple of times and have a period of silence to reflect. Depending on the group you may just want to share things, with someone writing them up on a flip chart or equivalent, or you may want to prepare a wall with large sheets of paper where people can write things up under the heading 'Signs of the Times'. Another possibility is to use newspapers, magazines, etc. with people cutting out pictures and headlines that strike them. The important issue here isn't really identifying the signs, it is knowing how to interpret them. This may be teased out as we reflect on questions such as:

• What do these signs say to us about what we should be doing?
• Where should we be putting our energies?
• What may the next six months/year bring that we need to plan for now?
• How should what we have discovered affect our approach to mission and ministry?
• Should we change anything as a result of our reflections?
• If we identify action what do we need to learn, do, become and so on to enable us to take that action?

For further reflection
Use the following to trigger your own reflection:

• War in Africa – soldiers cut women's breasts off so that they could not feed their babies.
• God gave us good weather/a car parking space.
• A new experiment where there are no road markings – pedestrians have to make eye contact to cross the road.

The clearness committee

As with many of the ideas in this book this one could have gone in other chapters, particularly Chapter 4 on spiritual practices. However, we have left it here to emphasize the benefits of a group approach to spiritual discernment. As we have grown older we have become more appreciative of Quaker customs and traditions; silence is more appealing now than it was in our twenties where it just seemed weird! Parker J. Palmer is one of Sally's significant influences. It is through his work that we first became aware of the Quaker practice of clearness committees. We resonate with his experience in trying to deal with personal dilemmas and so often find that:

access to our own resources is often blocked by layers of inner 'stuff' – confusion, habitual thinking, fear, despair. On the other hand, we know that friends might help us uncover our inner resources and find our way, but by exposing our problem to others, we run the risk of being invaded and overwhelmed by their assumptions, judgments and advice – a common and alienating experience.

<http://www.broadwayumc.org/publications/
The_Clearness_Committee.pdf>

The idea of a clearness committee is that it helps us uncover our inner voice by helping to remove the interference. The person who is seeking clearance draws together a committee of five or six people who they trust but who ideally bring a range of perspectives. The focus person writes up their issue or dilemma and sends it out to people in advance of the meeting. This paper contains three main elements: a statement of the problem, identification of any relevant background material and any hunches about the issue.

The committee meets for two to three hours although it may be necessary to have one or two more meetings. One person is given responsibility for the timings of the meetings, adherence to the rules and another should record the meeting either digitally or by taking notes. The meeting begins with centring silence with the focus person breaking the silence when they are ready. Committee members may then speak but only to ask questions, which must be honest and open. No sharing of stories, possible interpretations and other temptations we often succumb to in our encounters are permitted. Questions should not be loaded and should help the focus person rather than satisfying curiosity. Ask what occurs to you and trust your intuition in the questioning. The focus person answers the questions (although he or she is free not to and is the one who establishes the boundaries of what is to be shared) and these often generate further questions. The pace of the questions should be relaxed; it is not a court room or tribunal. If silence occurs then don't be concerned as it is often out of silence that the deepest insights emerge. The attention needs to remain on the focus person and the situation is unlike usual social gatherings.

Twenty minutes before the end of the agreed time, the clerk should ask the focus person if he or she wants the committee to mirror back what they think they have heard and suspend the questions-only rule. In the last five minutes, members of the committee should offer affirmative comments to the focus person. What usually happens is that the individual who called the committee continues processing the issues beyond the initial experience.

Palmer concludes that a clearness committee can:

> become a way to free people from their isolation without threatening their integrity, a way to counteract the excesses of technique in caring, a way to create space for the spirit to move among us with healing and with power.
>
> <http://www.broadwayumc.org/publications/
> The_Clearness_Committee.pdf>

Palmer also suggests that this exercise can be done as part of a group retreat with a ten-minute oral introduction and a session lasting up to two hours.

Open Space Technology

Most of us spend hours in meetings and wonder why or what has been accomplished, or whether there are ways of making them more interesting and reflective. Originated by Harrison Owen, Open Space Technology (OST) is a different way of meeting and empowers those present to ensure that their voices are heard and their agendas explored. A website <www.openspaceworld.org> provides all you need to know. For us an event that sounds like this is attractive:

> It's been called passion bounded by responsibility, the energy of a good coffee break, intentional self-organization, spirit at work, chaos and creativity, evolution in organization, and a simple, powerful way to get people and organizations moving – when and where it's needed most.
>
> (Herman, 2008)

OST works only when the answer is not already known and works best when a diverse group of people need to work with complex material where a range of opinions exists (Owen, 1997, p. 15). The process can last anything between an hour and three days and has been used with groups of all sizes including one thousand plus participants. There are four principles and one law that underpin the process. The principles are:

- whoever comes are the right people
- whatever happens is the only thing that could have
- whenever it starts is the right time
- when it's over, it's over.

We may want to critique the first of these principles in light of good equal opportunities practice but if the work is done first about who should be invited and we ensure we are inclusive and creative then it is less of an issue. The one rule, the law of two feet, says if you are not learning or contributing then leave and find somewhere else where you can be productive (Owen, 1997, pp. 95–9).

The process has the following stages:

- Decide a focus and state it as a question, for example: What are the challenges facing St Faith's over the next five years? or, How can we engage with young people in our community?
- Issue an open invitation to those who might be interested. OST is about voluntary self-selection. Invitations should spark the imagination but also contain the necessary information about venue, date, time, etc. Don't explain OST but say that though it may be new in our context, it has been used all over the world to great effect.
- For the event, arrange the chairs in a circle or other appropriate shape and have a large wall space. You will need plenty of masking tape, sheets of paper, flip charts and pens. You will also need breakout spaces or rooms, each of which needs a flip chart; the number depends on the size of the group. Ideally there should be some computers available to type up summaries of the discussions.
- The facilitator then asks participants to share topics or issues they would like to discuss. These are written on a sheet of paper and stuck up on a wall. The group then agrees a timetable that ensures that all of the topics are covered and a time and venue assigned. Ideally the person who suggests the topic facilitates the group and any combining of topics needs to be carefully negotiated between those who suggested them. If having an event lasting more than half a day, you may want to schedule other opportunities to suggest topics.
- The discussion for each topic should be recorded in some way and the results put in a public place so participants can get an idea of what is emerging.
- A final session is held in the circle to reflect on the process; identify the ideas, themes, issues, findings that have emerged from the process; and agree an action plan for the way forward. The

reports from all the discussions should be collated and distributed to participants.

Both the OST website and Owen (1997) guide you through the process in great detail. The process doesn't guarantee coming to a common mind but it should help identify all the issues; the action plan may involve revisiting various facets of the conversation to try to reach a consensus eventually.

The World Café

> In every World Café, there's a wonderful feeling of invitation. Attention is paid to creating hospitable space. But the hospitality runs much deeper. It is rooted in the host's awareness that everyone is needed, that anyone may contribute that something that suddenly sparks a collective insight. (Wheatley in Brown and Isaacs, 2005, p. x)

We went to the Malt Cross, a café bar in the middle of Nottingham, for a conference on the future of youth work organized by Frontier Youth Trust and Worth Unlimited. There were many people there including students, youth workers, advisers and educationalists from a range of contexts. In one day a group of people got together and creatively, passionately explored the topic. There was a sense of energy, empowerment and excitement as we explored together. The World Café is about conversations that matter. It is based on a premise that within us we have the wisdom and creativity to deal with even the most complex issues or challenges (Brown and Isaacs, 2005, p. 4). In essence, a question is identified, and there are a series of rounds of conversation around small tables to discuss different elements of that question. Individuals are free to move from table to table at the end of each round, taking with them the insights from the last conversation. There is normally a summary session at the end of the day that seeks to draw everything together.

There are seven principles of the World Café process (adapted from Brown and Isaacs, 2005):

Principle 1 Set the context

There are three elements of the context that need to be agreed: the purpose, the participants and the parameters.

Principle 2 Create hospitable space

The room should be set up to look like a café and ideally given a name. Language such as hosts, guests, and travellers helps create the right atmosphere, as does giving gifts, or using special language and metaphors, such as planting seeds and cross-pollinating ideas. Café etiquette should be explained:

- Contribute your thinking and experience.
- Listen to understand.
- Connect ideas.
- Listen together for patterns, insights, and deeper questions.
- Play, doodle, draw!

Principle 3 Explore questions that matter

Unlike OST, here the host(s) develop the questions. These guidelines help in developing and refining the questions:

- What question, if explored thoroughly, could provide the break-through possibilities we are seeking?
- Is the question relevant to the real life or real work of the people who will be exploring it?
- What work do I want this question to do? That is, what kind of conversation, meanings and feelings do I imagine this question will evoke in those who will be exploring it?
- What assumptions or beliefs are embedded in the way this question is constructed?
- Is this question likely to generate hope, imagination, engagement, new thinking and creative action, or is it likely to increase a focus on past problems and obstacles?
- Does this question leave room for new and different questions to be raised as the initial question is explored?

Principle 4 Encourage everyone's contribution

The challenge here is: 'What if your contribution is a key ingredient?' Experience from those involved in the World Café process suggests that rather than focusing on empowerment and participation, it is more beneficial to honour and encourage each person's unique contribution. Working out how to do that is a challenge for the hosts.

Principle 5 Cross-pollinate and connect diverse perspectives

If we ensure a diversity of participants we bring a greater variety of perspectives. Participants then move from table to table linking and connecting thoughts and developing networks of conversations. Various people use the word 'magic' to describe the synergy and creativity that emerges from the insight.

Principle 6 Listen together for patterns, insights, and deeper questions

At various points in a World Café, it is necessary to slow down and reflect and during the conversations music or poetry, for example, can be used to encourage a couple of minutes of quiet time when people make notes on Post-its or cards, which summarize their key thoughts in a conversation. Prompts can include:

- What did you most appreciate about this conversation?
- What's the real meaning for you from what you've heard? What surprised you? What challenged you?
- What's missing from the picture so far? What is it we're not seeing? What do we need more clarity about?
- If there were one thing that hadn't yet been explored but was necessary in order to reach a deeper level of understanding/clarity, what would that be?

The cards or Post-its are collected at the end of each round of conversation.

Principle 7 Harvest and share collective discoveries

Because insights from conversations can be lost it is important to try to work out ways of sharing these with the whole group. One idea is to have tablecloths you can write on, and doing a tour of the tables enables you to grasp much of what has happened. In large groups each person can contribute a significant idea and post it on a wall. You can start people in pairs, get them to join another couple and so on. You can give people dots to put alongside the question or issue they think is the most important. Ideally a report or summary should be produced and disseminated as soon as possible after the event. A reflection at the end of the World Café concludes, 'Together, we create a future worth living', which is surely part of what ministry is about.

Open Space Technology and the World Café are two of a number of processes that can be used to stimulate group reflection, particularly in large groups.

Conclusion

Dietrich Bonhoeffer writes eloquently about *Life Together* (1954) and effective life together is likely to be enhanced by reflecting together. We hope the ideas in this chapter and others will equip you to fulfil more of what it means to be church and Christian, living in community engaging with its environment and faith. We are a community of co-learners (Rogers, 1993) and together we work out God's desires and will for the kingdom to be expressed in our context.

? *What skills do I need to develop to become more effective in facilitating reflecting together?*

Afterword

Good days bad days

Father – on the good days the reality of your presence is
*   revealed in*
seemingly insignificant and commonplace things
I see you in a distant shoreline
and hear you in a curlew's evening call
Stooping to dead-head, a familiar-forgotten fragrance
transforms the border into a place of resurrection.
There are echoes of your Word
in the easy conversation of a friend
and healing in the laughter of a loved one.
There is time to gaze,
to ponder
to recount,
To explore a new desire for you.

(Farrell in Watterson, 2006, p. 45)

Children were lined up in the school cafeteria for lunch. At the head of the table was a large pile of apples. There was a note by the apples: 'Take only one, God is watching.' The children moved along to the other end of the table, where there was a large pile of chocolate chip biscuits. A boy wrote a note: 'Take all you want, God is watching the apples.'

Being reflective ministers

We are drawn to different sources for reflection, which is why we started this chapter with a poem and a joke. They don't seem to fit together but both lend themselves to some interesting reflections. While reading the poem, Sally was transported back to her favourite places, the restorative, recharging places. The joke reminded Paul that our constructs of God are not always healthy or life-giving but that being able to laugh in the midst of everything is essential.

163

We were watching a television programme. We no longer re-member what it was, but these lines stuck with us:

'Why did you do that?'
'I don't know. When I know, I'll let you know.'

That's what reflection offers us – a way of processing potential answers to the questions we need to ask and these may range from the small and seemingly insignificant to the big and profound issues that face us all. We can reflect on anything and use anything, as hope-fully this book has shown; the mundane, the shocking, the challeng-ing, the profound. Reflective ministry requires a theology that God seeks to speak and engage with us in and through everyday experi-ences and encounters. Reflective processes can be undergirded with prayer. We invite God into our reflection for his presence to accom-pany us, his wisdom to guide us and his perspective to enlighten us. God can be our companion on our reflective journey as can others. We recommend reflection done both prayerfully and habitually.

Reflecting helps us in our task of being lifelong learners. Our world changes so fast that what we learnt even a couple of years ago may not be what we need for the current situation. Initial training for a job or role is not enough; we need to continue to learn. Reflection helps us in being aware and developing self-awareness; we learn more about God, ourselves and our world as we reflect. We apply our critical skills to our experiences. Reflection as a habitual practice comes from asking such questions as, 'What can I learn about min-istry from what is around me?' and, 'What about ministry helps me to engage with and interpret the world around me?' It is enhanced by using all of our senses, not just the ones we most readily rely on. It can be enriched by drawing resources from areas such as socio-logy, psychology, leadership, business and science as well as theology.

We both draw on theories such as the Myers Briggs® Type Indicator and Transactional Analysis. We have not included them in this book as they need fuller explanations than we have space for if we are to understand them as tools. We need to remember the stages of interacting, interpreting and applying, giving due time to each stage. At times reflection requires us to be self-disciplined, to put other things down and focus on the task at hand instead of multitasking. We can take risks with our starting points and finishing places and expect to be surprised. We may also challenge others. At times it can feel as though the consequences of theological reflection lead us to being a prophetic voice in the wilderness.

We need to be honest and real as reflective ministers. We may need to ask ourselves: 'What has happened to me that helps me understand and respond in this situation?' We may ask: 'What is going on?' but sometimes we need to go deeper and ask: 'What is really going on?' as the superficial answer isn't adequate. Reflection should help us face our fears, our undesirable thoughts, the things we put on the back-burner, and to face and process hassles. Reflective processes give us different perspectives when we are stuck in a situation; we can see whether reflection brings a fresh insight or suggests a way forward.

We hope you will be inspired to have a go at the different exercises in this book but also to amend or change them to suit you and your context. The purpose of a tool is to help you do a job. A tool on its own is not much use; it only proves its worth when applied to a particular context – and imagination can lead to any number of contexts. We are not really into DIY and do not have many tools and therefore sometimes have to make do. We have probably all been frustrated and sometimes amused as we have tried to use a particular tool to achieve a task for which it was not designed. With many jobs we need more than one tool and similarly some situations or issues merit looking at from a range of perspectives or require us to hear from more than one voice. When choosing our tools we need to remember that there is no such thing as unbiased reflection and we need to be aware of our bias, presuppositions and assumptions as they can alter both the inputs and outcomes of our reflective processes.

End of the journey

Hopefully this book has provided you with a myriad ways and insights into being a theologically reflective minister. Our aim has been to encourage an approach which develops self-awareness, effectiveness, creativity, and a deeper sense of vocation as well as giving a range of tools and ideas which can be used with others to encourage their growth and development too.

Finishing writing a book can feel like finding the pot of gold at the end of the rainbow; time is redeemed, new ideas and opportunities can begin to take shape. Finishing reading a book is more interesting; many books have the capacity to change us but that often requires deliberate action. Our hope is that you now have reflection written on your to-do list and that you will be encouraged, amazed, inspired, challenged, transformed, reassured and blessed as a consequence. Some final questions:

- Which tools do you want to pack for the next part of your journey?
- What might you do differently?
- Have you learnt anything about yourself or your ministry that you need to do something about?
- In what ways has or can reflection become habitual and intuitive?

Enjoy the journey but take your toolbox (or perhaps, for ease and accessibility, a utility belt) with you!

Bibliography

Alcott, L. M. *Little Women*. London: Penguin Modern Classics, 1997.

Allen, P. B. *Art is a Way of Knowing*. Boston: Shambhala, 1995.

Arthur, S. *The God-Hungry Imagination*. Nashville: Upper Room Books, 1997.

Atkinson, T. and Claxton, G., eds. *The Intuitive Practitioner*. Maidenhead: Open University Press, 2003.

Augsburger, D. W. *Helping People Forgive*. Louisville: Westminster John Knox, 1996.

Axline, V. *Dibs in Search of Self*. London: Penguin, 1990.

Bach, R. *Jonathan Livingston Seagull*. Basingstoke: Macmillan, 1973.

Balding, R. *Nineplus*. Truro: Nineplus Ltd, 2007.

Ballard, P. and Pritchard, J. *Practical Theology in Action*. London: SPCK, 1996.

Barber, V. *Explore Yourself Through Art*. London: Carroll & Brown, 2002.

Bennett, D. *Nine O'Clock in the Morning*. Eastbourne: Kingsway, 1974.

Bennett, D. W. *Metaphors of Ministry*. Carlisle: Paternoster Press, 1993.

Bergmann, S. *God in Context: A Survey of Contextual Theology*. Aldershot: Ashgate, 2003.

Bevans, S. B. *Models of Contextual Theology*, revised edition. Maryknoll: Orbis, 2002.

Blythe, T. A. *50 Ways to Pray*. Nashville: Abingdon Press, 2006.

Bonhoeffer, D. *The Cost of Discipleship*. London: SCM, 2001.

Bonhoeffer, D. *Life Together*. London: SCM, 1954.

Boud, D., Cohen, R. and Walker, D., eds. *Using Experience for Learning*. Buckingham: Open University Press, 1993.

Boud, D., Cressey, P. and Docherty, P., eds. *Productive Reflection at Work*. Abingdon: Routledge, 2006.

Brain, P. *Going the Distance*. Kingsford: Matthias Media, 2004.

Brook, P. A. *Religion, Art and the Australian Landscape: A visual and verbal exploration of the landscape as symbol of identity and place of belonging and as a site and source of understanding and meaning*. Unpublished PhD, University of Newcastle, Newcastle, Australia, 2006.

Brookfield, S. D. *Becoming a Critically Reflective Practitioner*. San Francisco: Jossey-Bass, 1995.

Brother Lawrence. *The Practice of the Presence of God*. Mineola: Dover Publications, 2005.

Brown, J. and Isaacs, D. *The World Café*. San Francisco: Berrett Koehler, 2005.

Browne, D. 'Films, movies, meanings'. In *Explorations in Theology and Film*, C. Marsh and G. Ortiz, eds. Oxford: Blackwell, 1997.

Bibliography

Buzan, T. *The Ultimate Book of Mind Maps*. London: HarperCollins, 2005.

Calhoun, A. A. *Spiritual Disciplines Handbook*. Downers Grove: InterVarsity Press, 2005.

Cameron, J. *The Vein of Gold*. London: Pan, 1996.

Carter, W. J. *Team Spirituality*. Nashville: Abingdon Press, 1997.

Claiborne, S. *The Irresistible Revolution: Living as an Ordinary Radical*. Grand Rapids: Zondervan, 2006.

Claxton, G. 'The anatomy of intuition'. In *The Intuitive Practitioner*, T. Atkinson and G. Claxton, eds. Maidenhead: Open University Press, 2003.

Cochrane, J. R. *Circles of Dignity*. Minneapolis: Fortress Press, 1999.

Cole, B. *That's Why!* St Helen's: Ted Smart, 2006.

Covey, S. *The 7 Habits of Highly Effective People*. London: Simon & Schuster, 1989.

Cressey, P., Boud, D. and Docherty, P. 'The emergence of productive reflection'. In *Productive Reflection at Work*, D. Boud, P. Cressey and P. Docherty, eds. (pp. 11–26). Abingdon: Routledge, 2006.

Dalley, T., ed. *Art as Therapy*. Hove: Brunner-Routledge, 1984.

Darley, S. and Heath, W. *Expressive Arts Activity Book*. London: Jessica Kingsley, 2008.

de Bary, E. O. *Theological Reflection*. Collegeville: Liturgical Press, 2003.

Dewey, J. *How We Think*. Boston: Houghton Mifflin Company, 1933.

Drane, J. *After McDonaldization*. London: Darton, Longman & Todd, 2008.

Dunn, W. *Living Sensationally: Understanding Your Senses*. London: Jessica Kingsley, 2008.

Dwinell, M. *Being Priest to One Another*. Ligouri: Triumph Books, 1993.

Ensley, E. and Herrmann, R. *Writing to be Whole*. Chicago: Loyola Press, 2001.

Evans, D. *Practice Learning in the Caring Professions*. Aldershot: Ashgate, 1999.

Farber-Robertson, A. *Learning While Leading: Increasing your Effectiveness in Ministry*. Herndon: Alban Institute, 2000.

Fleming, N. *VARK Learning Styles*. <http://www.vark-learn.com/english/page.asp?p=questionnaire>, 2001–2006, accessed 23 June 2008.

Fook, J. and Gardner, F. *Practising Critical Reflection*. Maidenhead: Open University Press, 2007.

Frost, M. *Seeing God in the Ordinary*. Peabody: Hendrickson, 2000.

Gardner, H. *Five Minds for the Future*. Boston: Harvard Business School Press, 2006.

Gardner, H. *Intelligence Reframed: Multiple Intelligences for the 21st Century*. New York: Basic Books, 2000.

Gill, R. *Theology and Sociology: A Reader*. London: Continuum, 1996.

Goff, K. I. *Active Spirituality*. Herndon: Alban Institute, 1993.

Goldman, C. and Dols, W. *Finding Jesus, Discovering Self*. Harrisburg: Morehouse Publishing, 2006.

Bibliography

Goodman, D. *Impossibly Beautiful*. CD distributed by ICC. Cambridge: Note for a Child, 2003.

Graham, E., Walton, H. and Ward, F. *Theological Reflection: Methods*. London: SCM, 2005.

Green, B. *Like a Tree Planted*. Collegeville: Liturgical Press, 1997.

Green, L. *Let's Do Theology*. London: Mowbray, 1990.

Greenwood, R. *Transforming Priesthood*. London: SPCK, 1994.

Grothe, M. *I Never Metaphor I Didn't Like*. New York: HarperCollins, 2008.

Halverson, D. *Meditations by the Sea*. Kelowna: Northstone Publishing, 1999.

Herman, M. *What is Open Space Technology?* <http://www.openspaceworld. org/cgi/wiki.cgi?AboutOpenSpace>, 1998, accessed 30 September 2008.

Hieb, M. *Inner Journeying Through Art-Journaling*. London: Jessica Kingsley, 2005.

Hillier, Y. *Reflective Teaching in Further and Adult Education*. London: Continuum, 2002.

Hodgson, J. *The Faith We See*. Peterborough: Inspire, 2006.

Holman, B. *Kids at the Door*. Oxford: Blackwell, 1984.

Honey, P. and Mumford, A. *The Manual of Learning Styles*. Maidenhead: Peter Honey, 1992.

Johns, C. *Becoming a Reflective Practitioner*, 2nd edition. Oxford: Blackwell, 2004.

Jones, K. B. *Holy Play*. San Francisco: Jossey-Bass, 2007.

Julian of Norwich. *Showing of Love* (J. B. Holloway, trans.). Collegeville: Liturgical Press, 2003.

Keller, P. *Sea Edge*. Waco: Word Books, 1985.

Kettering, T. *The Elephant in the Room*. <http://www.goodgriefresources.com/ poems/griefpoem16.htm>, accessed 23 December 2008.

Killen, P. O. and de Beer, J. *The Art of Theological Reflection*. New York: Crossroad, 1999.

Kinast, R. L. *Let Ministry Teach*. Collegeville, Minnesota: Liturgical Press, 1996.

Kinast, R. L. *What Are They Saying About Theological Reflection?* New York: Paulist Press, 2000.

Klug, R. *How to Keep a Spiritual Journal*, revised edition. Minneapolis: Augsburg, 2002.

Kolb, D. A. *Experiential Learning*. Englewood Cliffs: Prentice Hall, 1984.

Kolb, D. A. 'The process of experiential learning'. In *Culture and Processes of Adult Learning*, M. Thorpe, R. Edwards and A. Hanson, eds. London: Routledge, 1993 (original chapter, 1984).

Lakoff, G. and Johnson, M. *Metaphors We Live By*. Chicago: University of Chicago Press, 1980.

Lamdin, K. and Tilley, D. *Supporting New Ministers in the Local Church*. London: SPCK, 2007.

Bibliography

Leckey, D. R. *7 Essentials for the Spiritual Journey*. New York: Crossroad, 1999.

Leder, D. *Sparks of the Divine*. Notre Dame: Sorin Books, 2004.

Leech, K. *Soul Friend*. London: Darton, Longman & Todd, 1994.

Lewis, C. *The Weight of Glory*. <http://www.doxaweb.com/assets/doxa.pdf>, accessed 25 July 2008.

Liebmann, M. *Art Therapy for Groups*, 2nd edition. Hove: Brunner-Routledge, 2004.

Linn, D., Fabricant Linn, S. and Linn, M. *Sleeping with Bread*. Mahwah: Paulist Press, 1995.

Lynch, G. ed. *Between Sacred and Profane*. London: I. B. Tauris, 2007.

MacBeth, S. *Praying in Color*. Brewster: Paraclete Press, 2007.

MacDonald, A. *Films in Close-up*. Leicester: IVP, 1991.

McFague, S. *Speaking in Parables*. London: SCM, 1975.

McGrath, A. E. *Christian Theology: An Introduction*. Oxford: Blackwell, 1994.

Mahan, J. H. 'Reflections on the Past and Future'. In *Between Sacred and Profane*, G. Lynch, ed. London: I. B. Tauris, 2007.

Malchiodi, C. A. *The Art Therapy Sourcebook*. Lincolnwood: Lowell House, 1998.

Marsh, C. *Cinema and Sentiment*. Carlisle: Paternoster, 2004.

Marsh, C. and Ortiz, G. eds. *Explorations in Theology and Film*. Oxford: Blackwell, 1997.

Miller, T. *The Heretical Imperative*. Chatton: Northumberland Community Trust, 2003.

Monbourquette, J. *How to Discover Your Personal Mission*. London: Darton, Longman & Todd, 2003.

Moon, J. A. *A Handbook of Reflective and Experiential Learning*. Abingdon: RoutledgeFalmer, 2004.

Moon, J. A. *Reflection in Learning and Professional Development*. London: Kogan Page, 2000.

Nash, P. *What Theology for Youth Work?* Cambridge: Grove Books, 2007.

Nash, S. *Sustaining Your Spirituality*. Cambridge: Grove Books, 2006.

Nash, S. *A Theology for Urban Youth Work*. Cambridge: YTC Press, 2008.

Nash, S., Pimlott, J. and Nash, P. *Skills for Collaborative Ministry*. London: SPCK, 2008.

Nelson, W. R. *Ministry Formation for Effective Leadership*. Nashville: Abingdon Press, 1988.

Niebuhr, R. *Christ and Culture*. New York: Harper, 1951.

Northumbria Community. *Celtic Daily Prayer*. London: HarperCollins, 2000.

Nouwen, H. J. M. *Creative Ministry*. New York: Image, 1971.

Nouwen, H. J. M. *A Cry for Mercy*. New York: Doubleday, 1981.

Nouwen, H. J. M. *The Genesee Diary: Report from a Trappist Monastery*. New York: Doubleday, 1976.

Bibliography

Nouwen, H. J. M. *The Inner Voice of Love: A Journey through Anguish to Freedom*. New York: Doubleday, 1996.

Nouwen, H. J. M. *Jesus: A Gospel*. Maryknoll: Orbis, 2001.

Nouwen, H. J. M. *Reaching Out*. London: Fount, 1980.

Nouwen, H. J. M. *The Wounded Healer*. London: Darton, Longman & Todd, 1994.

O'Leary, D. J. *New Hearts, New Models*. Dublin: Columba Press, 1997.

Orbach, S. *Fat is a Feminist Issue*. Feltham: Hamlyn, 1978.

Osborn, L. *Paper Pilgrimage*. London: Daybreak, 1990.

Owen, H. *Open Space Technology*. San Francisco: Berrett-Koehler, 1997.

Oxford English Dictionary. *Metaphor*. <www.dictionary.oed.com>, accessed 14 October 2008.

Palmer, P. J. *The Clearness Committee: A Communal Approach to Discernment*. <http://www.broadwayumc.org/publications/The_Clearness_Committee.pdf>, accessed 29 September 2008.

Palmer, P. J. *A Hidden Wholeness*. San Francisco: Jossey-Bass, 2004.

Parkin, M. *Tales for Trainers*. London: Kogan Page, 1998.

Paver, J. E. *Theological Reflection and Education for Ministry*. Aldershot: Ashgate, 2006.

Pennell, A. E. and Browne, K. D. Film violence and young offenders. *Aggression and Violent Behaviour*, 4(1):13–28, 1999.

Percy, M. *Engaging with Contemporary Culture*. Aldershot: Ashgate, 2005.

Peterson, E. H. *The Message*. Colorado Springs: Navpress, 2002.

Pritchard, J. *The Life and Work of a Priest*. London: SPCK, 2007.

Rogers, C. R. 'The interpersonal relationship in the facilitation of learning'. In *Culture and Processes of Adult Learning*, M. Thorpe *et al.* eds. London: Routledge, 1993.

Rolfe, G., Freshwater, D. and Jasper, M. *Critical Reflection for Nursing and the Helping Professions*. Basingstoke: Palgrave, 2001.

Rupp, J. *Dear Heart, Come Home*. New York: Crossroad, 1996.

Rupp, J. *Inviting God In*. Notre Dame: Ave Maria Press, 2001.

Ryle, J. C. *Holiness*. Cambridge: J. Clarke, 1952.

Sanders, J. O. *Spiritual Leadership*. Bromley: STL Books, 1981.

Savage, S., Collins-Mayo, S., Mayo, B. and Cray, G. *Making Sense of Generation Y*. London: Church House Publishing, 2006.

Schon, D. *The Reflective Practitioner*. New York: Basic Books, 1983.

Schutz, W. *FIRO: A Three Dimensional Theory of Interpersonal Behavior*. New York: Holt, Rinehart & Winston, 1958.

Seddon, J. *Meditations by the Sea*. Tilbury: Apostleship of the Sea, undated.

Simpson, R. and Lyons Lee, B. *Emerging Downunder*. Adelaide: ATF Press, 2008.

Sine, T. *Why Settle for More and Miss the Best?* Carlisle: Paternoster, 1989.

Smith, M. D. *Journal Keeper*. Grand Rapids: Eerdmans, 1992.

Smyth, J. 'Developing socially critical educators'. In *Working with Experience*, D. Boud and N. Miller, eds. London: Routledge, 1996.

Snow, J. *Moments and Thoughts*. London: Kaye & Ward, 1973.

Sofield, L., Hammett, R. and Juliano, C. *Building Community*. Notre Dame: Ave Maria Press, 1998.

Solzhenitsyn, A. *One Day in the Life of Ivan Denisovich*. London: Penguin, 2000.

Sunderland, M. and Engleheart, P. *Draw on Your Emotions*. Bicester: Speechmark, 1993.

Thompson, N. *People Skills*. Basingstoke: Macmillan, 1996.

Thompson, N. *Promoting Equality*. Basingstoke: Palgrave Macmillan, 1998.

Ward, P. *Participation and Mediation*. London: SCM, 2008.

Ward, P. *Selling Worship: How What We Sing Has Changed the Church*. Carlisle: Paternoster, 2005.

Watterson, S. ed. *Looking Through Glass*. Dublin: Veritas Publications, 2006.

Watts, F. N. *Theology and Psychology*. Aldershot: Ashgate, 2002.

Watts, F., Nye, R. and Savage, S. *Psychology for Christian Ministry*. London: Routledge, 2001.

Wenger, E. *Communities of Practice*. Cambridge: Cambridge University Press, 1998.

Wenger, E. Communities of Practice. <http://www.ewenger.com/theory/>, accessed 29 September 2008.

Whitcomb, H. W. *Practicing Your Path*. Philadelphia: Innisfree Press, 2002.

Whitehead, J. D. and Whitehead, E. E. *Christian Adulthood*. Liguori: Liguori Publishing, 2005.

Whitehead, J. D. and Whitehead, E. E. *Method in Ministry*. Franklin, Wisconsin: Sheed & Ward, 1995.

Widdicombe, C. *Small Communities in Religious Life: Making Them Work*. Cambridge: Lutterworth Press, 2001.

Wild Goose Worship Group. *Iona Abbey Worship Book*. Glasgow: WGWG, 2001.

Williams, R. *The Christian Priest Today*: lecture on the occasion of the 150th Anniversary of Ripon College, Cuddesdon, 28 May 2004. <http://www.archbishopofcanterbury.org/1185>, accessed 14 November 2008.

Young, W. P. *The Shack*. London: Hodder & Stoughton, 2008.

Websites

<www.businessballs.com> user-friendly summaries of management and other theories and ideas for icebreakers, etc.

<www.ewenger.com> Etienne Wenger's website with accessible material on Communities of Practice.

Further reading

Introduction

Ensley, E. and Herrmann, R. *Writing to be Whole*. Chicago: Loyola Press, 2001.
Exercises to help us process some of the issues we face that may inhibit our
capacity for ministry.

Honey, P. and Mumford, A. *The Manual of Learning Styles*. Maidenhead: Peter
Honey, 1992.

Klug, R. *How to Keep a Spiritual Journal*, revised edition. Minneapolis:
Augsburg, 2002.
Practical, lots of resources and realistic about problems.

Nouwen, H. J. M. *The Genesee Diary: Report from a Trappist Monastery*. New
York: Doubleday, 1976.
Challengingly honest account of Nouwen's stay in a Trappist monastery.

Watts, F., Nye, R. and Savage, S. *Psychology for Christian Ministry*. London:
Routledge, 2001.
Helpful insights and discussions on issues which may be raised through
reflection.

1 Being reflective

Gardner, H. *Five Minds for the Future*. Boston: Harvard Business School Press,
2006.
Inspiring read that encourages us to develop in ways that will equip us for
the future.

Johns, C. *Becoming a Reflective Practitioner*, 2nd edition. Oxford: Blackwell,
2004.
Comprehensive introduction, written predominantly for nurses but easily
transferable.

Moon, J. A. *Reflection in Learning and Professional Development*. London: Kogan
Page, 2000.
Excellent overview of the concept of reflective practice.

2 Being theologically reflective

Ballard, P. and Pritchard, J. *Practical Theology in Action*. London: SPCK,
1996.
Good overview of different approaches to practical theology including
theological reflection.

Graham, E., Walton, H. and Ward, F. *Theological Reflection: Methods*.
London: SCM, 2005.

British-written, well-referenced introduction to a variety of ways of doing theological reflection.

Paver, J. E. *Theological Reflection and Education for Ministry*. Aldershot: Ashgate, 2006.

Australian-written discussion of the role of theological reflection in ministry development, particularly as part of initial training.

Whitehead, J. D. and Whitehead, E. E. *Method in Ministry*. Franklin, Wisconsin: Sheed & Ward, 1995.

US-written insightful discussion of ways of reflecting on ministry that pays attention to culture.

3 Using metaphor in reflection

Bennett, D. W. *Metaphors of Ministry*. Carlisle: Paternoster Press, 1993.

Helpful exposition of a range of mainly biblical metaphors for ministry.

Green, B. *Like a Tree Planted*. Collegeville: Liturgical Press, 1997.

Reflections on psalms and parables through metaphor, one of each on different themes.

Grothe, M. *I Never Metaphor I Didn't Like*. New York: HarperCollins, 2008.

Useful overview plus a myriad examples that help with creative reflection, writing, teaching and preaching.

Lakoff, G. and Johnson, M. *Metaphors We Live By*. Chicago: University of Chicago Press, 1980.

Very good theoretical overview with lots of insightful comments.

4 Spiritual practices for reflection

Blythe, T. A. *50 Ways to Pray*. Nashville: Abingdon Press, 2006.

Lots of creative ideas that can be adapted to suit our own context.

Calhoun, A. A. *Spiritual Disciplines Handbook*. Downers Grove: InterVarsity Press, 2005.

Good introductory overview, would be useful in preparing small group materials.

Foster, R. *Celebration of Discipline*. London: Hodder & Stoughton, 1980.

Classic, challenging, merits revisiting regularly.

McLaren, B. *Finding Our Way Again*. Nashville: Thomas Nelson, 2008.

Revisits spiritual disciplines from the perspective of someone in the emerging church movement.

5 Reframing the past, imagining the future, understanding the present

Hill, J. *The History of Christian Thought*. Oxford: Lion, 2003.

Accessible introduction to church history in one volume.

McGrath, A. E. *Christian Theology: An Introduction*, 4th edition. Oxford: Blackwell, 2006.

Useful introduction to the field for those who have not studied it previously.

Miles, M. R. *The Word Made Flesh: A History of Christian Thought*. Oxford: Blackwell, 2004.

More of an academic textbook but well written and with a CD giving lots of images.

6 Using culture in reflection

Arthur, S. *The God-Hungry Imagination*. Nashville: Upper Room Books, 1997.

Although written for youth workers, an excellent introduction to storytelling in contemporary culture.

Bevans, S. B. *Models of Contextual Theology*, revised edition. Maryknoll: Orbis, 2002.

Good introduction and overview of contextual theology.

Donovan, V. *Christianity Rediscovered*. London: SCM, 1982.

Classic book on mission and highly influential in youth work.

Drane, J. *After McDonaldization*. London: Darton, Longman & Todd, 2008.

Discussion on mission, ministry and discipleship in contemporary culture.

Newbigin, L. *The Gospel in a Pluralist Society*. London: SPCK, 1989.

Formative in helping people think about culture in a changing societal context.

Niebuhr, R. *Christ and Culture*. New York: Harper, 1951.

Classic often quoted by others that explores different positions we can take regarding culture.

Percy, M. *Engaging with Contemporary Culture*. Aldershot: Ashgate, 2005.

Challenging and compelling discussion at an academic level.

Ward, P. *Participation and Mediation*. London: SCM, 2008.

Subtitled 'a practical theology for the liquid church', this book demonstrates how to take both theology and culture seriously in a way that impacts our ministry.

7 Reflecting without words

Liebmann, M. *Art Therapy for Groups*. Hove: Routledge, 1986.

Practical and accessible, full of ideas and helpful advice.

Malchiodi, C. A. *The Art Therapy Sourcebook*. Lincolnwood: Lowell House, 1998.

Useful theory and concepts that can be adapted and applied into our context.

Sunderland, M. and Engleheart, P. *Draw On Your Emotions*. Bicester: Speechmark, 1993.

Very good resource for use with young people in particular. Lots of exercises to explore difficult issues.

8 Reflecting with nature

Frost, M. *Seeing God in the Ordinary*. Peabody: Hendrickson, 2000.
Excellent introduction to the concept of seeing God in the everyday.
Leder, D. *Sparks of the Divine*. Notre Dame: Sorin Books, 2004.
A very practical book which encourages us to see God in a variety of ways
and settings.

9 Reflecting together

Brown, J. and Isaacs, D. *The World Café*. San Francisco: Berrett-Koehler, 2005.
Summary of the technique with lots of stories and helpful hints as to how
to make World Café work.
Isaacs, W. *Dialogue and the Art of Thinking Together*. New York: Doubleday,
1999.
A detailed analysis of the benefits of dialogue, written for the business con-
text but with plenty of useful material for the ministry setting.
Nash, S., Pimlott, J. and Nash, P. *Skills for Collaborative Ministry*. London:
SPCK, 2008.
Useful resources to help you facilitate, work in groups and teams, handle
conflict, as well as other ministry skills.
Owen, H. *Open Space Technology*. San Francisco: Berrett-Koehler, 1997.
Introduction to OST by the person who created the process.
Pimlott, N. *Participative Processes*. Birmingham: Frontier Youth Trust, 2009.
Short, accessible introduction to a range of ways of reflecting together.
Widdicombe, C. *Small Communities in Religious Life: Making Them Work*.
Cambridge: Lutterworth Press, 2001.
Although written for intentional communities there are lots of ideas and con-
cepts that help ministry teams or other Christian groups reflect together.

Afterword

McGuinness, J. *Growing Spiritually with the Myers-Briggs® Model*. London:
SPCK, 2009.
An accessible introduction to how the Myers Briggs® Type Indicator can help
our spiritual growth.
Ramsay, G. G. and Sweet, H. B. *A Creative Guide to Exploring Your Life*. London:
Jessica Kingsley, 2008.
Not written from a Christian perspective but encourages self-reflection
through photography, art and writing.
Whitehead, J. D. and Whitehead, E. E. *Christian Adulthood*. Liguori: Liguori
Publishing, 2005.
Helpful exploration of important issues for ministry, such as personal
power, vocation, self-intimacy and stewardship.
Wiederkehr, M. *Seven Sacred Pauses*. Notre Dame: Sorin Books, 2008.
Lots of resources to help you live mindfully during the day.

Index of subjects and names

Index of tools and exercises

Index of tools and exercises